"Dave Martin understands what it takes to be great in life, and I am always challenged and lifted when I am with him. He inspires me to think new thoughts, take new paths, and make a difference. *Make That, Break That* proves he's one of the world's greatest communicators, having the ability to share deep insights and profound knowledge all while making us laugh. While the results you will receive are uncommon, the principles he shares in *Make That, Break That* are simple. If you practice them, they will ultimately change the trajectory of your life and business. I encourage you to lean in and learn something new."

—JOHN MAXWELL
New York Times Best-Selling Author, Voted
World's #1 Leadership Expert by *Inc.* Magazine

"I want to say, 'Thank You!' to Dr. Dave Martin. You are impacting the lives of all those you coach and minister to. I love your quote: "The Rest Of Your Life Will Be The Best of Your Life."

—DREW BREES
NFL Quarterback

"Dr. Dave is a great leader and cares deeply about people. He is full of wisdom and practical tips and will always leave you encouraged. He will help you become who God created you to be. I have known him for a long time, and he has made me better."

—JOEL OSTEEN
New York Times Best-Selling Author
and Pastor, Lakewood Church

"Dr. Dave Martin is an incredibly anointed life coach. He has one of the most powerful and profound messages I have ever heard. When you get around him, your life is going to another level. Dr. Dave is more than talk; he is a man of massive vision."

—JENTEZEN FRANKLIN
New York Times Best-Selling Author and
Senior Pastor, Free Chapel Church

"Dr. Dave is a man on fire! I'm blessed to call him a friend. Let me tell you, he has the information and the inspiration. He leads with vision. There is no better visionary gift than that of my good friend, Dr. Dave Martin."

—DEVON FRANKLIN
Hollywood Producer, Best-Selling Author

"Dr. Dave Martin is an incredible leader. I am grateful for him and the wisdom he shares. I couldn't recommend a better person!"

—BRIAN HOUSTON
Global Senior Pastor, Hillsong Church Leadership

"Dr. Dave Martin is one of the wisest men I know. He is genuine, sincere, and authentic. Who would not want to follow a leader like that? You can describe this man in three words: genius, genuine, and generous."

—DHARIUS DANIELS
Cultural Architect and Lead Pastor, Change Church

"Dr. Dave has a way of changing the way you look at things. And trust me, you will like what you see."

—JUDAH SMITH
Best-Selling Author and Lead Pastor, Churchome

"Dave Martin is an outstanding speaker, inspiring author, and impactful coach. His work impacts millions around the world. Dave is an amazing person—respected from border to border and from coast to coast. He'll bring you knowledge. He'll bring you vision. He's a hero, model, and mentor, but more importantly, he understands viscerally what each of us needs to grow while helping others in the process."

—NIDO QUBEIN
President, High Point University

"Life offers us many opportunities to win or lose in whatever we are trying to achieve. The difference between winning and losing is often one inch, one second, or one habit. Dr. Dave will teach you and convince you how to break the habits that don't serve you and create the habits that will lead you to success. Study *Make That, Break That*!"

—LEE COCKERELL
Former Executive Vice President, Walt Disney World

"Every boxing champion knows that the way to triumph is to take your hits and keep coming back. Life is the same—you have to keep coming back. Create the habits you need. *Make That, Break That* outlines the habits you need to go the distance. This book is the 'real deal.'"

—EVANDER HOLYFIELD
Five-Time Heavyweight Champion of the World

"Dave Martin's teaching has transformed not only me but also my family and business life. I appreciate his wisdom and incredible sense of humor. He captures your attention and allows you to create a new crease in your brain in regards to leadership."

—GILLIAN ORTEGA
Mary Kay, Inc.

MAKE

THAT,

**HOW TO BREAK BAD HABITS AND MAKE
NEW ONES THAT LEAD TO SUCCESS**

BREAK

THAT

DAVE MARTIN

INSPIRE

Scripture quotations marked KJV are taken from the King James Version of the Bible. Public domain. | Scripture quotations marked NIV are taken from the Holy Bible, New International Version®, NIV®. Copyright © 1973, 1978, 1984, 2011 by Biblica, Inc.™ Used by permission of Zondervan. All rights reserved worldwide. www.zondervan.com. The "NIV" and "New International Version" are trademarks registered in the United States Patent and Trademark Office by Biblica, Inc.™ Scripture quotations marked "ISV" or "ISV 2.0" are taken from The Holy Bible: International Standard Version® 2.0. U.S. English Imprint Release 2.0 Copyright © 1996-2012 The ISV Foundation all rights reserved internationally. Used by permission of Davidson Press, LLC. All rights reserved internationally. For foreign and subsidiary rights, contact the author.

Cover design: Joe DeLeon

ISBN: 978-1-954089-06-8   1 2 3 4 5 6 7 8 9 10

Printed in the United States of America

CONTENTS

INTRODUCTION

THIS BOOK IS ABOUT HABITS—GOOD HABITS AND bad habits. To help get us into the right frame of mind for this subject matter and to help you wrap your brain around the things I am going to share, I want you to travel with me back to your childhood. I want to explore an old, familiar children's story you probably heard when you were young. Over the years, I've heard different versions of this story, but it goes something like this:

There once was a little boy who had a lot of bad habits. The boy's teacher realized he needed to do something to teach the boy about the power of habits and the importance of developing good ones. Although the boy seemed to have a kind heart and was actually a good student, the teacher, out of concern for his student, started pondering what he might be able to do to help the boy avoid a lifetime of unpleasant consequences as a result of his bad habits.

After giving the problem some thought, the teacher, with the permission of the boy's parents, asked his young student to go for a walk with him one afternoon after school. He told the boy the purpose of the walk was to learn

9

some important lessons from nature. As the teacher and the young lad made their way along a beautiful nature trail near the school, the teacher asked the boy to pull up one of the little sprouts growing out of the ground. The boy completed the task with no difficulty whatsoever. A little later, the teacher asked the boy to pull up a small seedling. The boy had to use some muscle in order to pull, because the seedling was larger than the tiny sprout. However, he was still able to pull up the little shrub with relatively light effort.

After walking a little further and discussing the types of plants he had already encountered, the young lad received instructions from his teacher to pull up a very small tree near the pathway they were navigating. The little boy grabbed hold of the two-foot tree and pulled it with all his might, but the small sapling did not yield to his efforts. He tried again and again. Eventually, he was able to pull the small tree from the ground and pride-fully presented it to his teacher.

But then, as their journey was coming to a close, the teacher asked the boy to pull up a fully-grown tree. The boy laughed and jokingly wrapped his arms around the tree, pretending to make an effort to rip the tree from the soil. However, both the teacher and the student knew the tree would never yield to the little boy's efforts. The boy's attempts to uproot the tree were in vain.

That's when the teacher started talking to his young student about the power of habits. "The deeper the roots, the harder it is to pull the tree from the ground," the teacher said. "That's the way it is with our habits. Whether it's our good habits or our bad ones, they take root and they grow. Eventually they become almost impossible to remove from our lives. Like a *mighty oak tree in the forest, they tower above all the rest of the plants and shrubs, and they cast their shadow over everything that happens under the influence of their spreading boughs."*

This story is the reason I have written this book. Most of us have no idea how many habits we have. At some point in our lives, we learned these behaviors, and we found them to be enjoyable, helpful, or rewarding in some way. Because of this, we continued to do them until they became fixtures in our lives. They became routine and thus became permanent, and we did them without thinking and without putting forth any effort to perform them.

If this sounds like you, you're not alone. Scientists tell us about half our daily activities are habitual in nature. In other words, as the dictionary states, they are "settled" or part of a "regular tendency or practice, especially one that is hard to give up." In other words, we perform our habits without actually planning to do them. We perform them without trying to do them. We perform them without even thinking about them or reminding ourselves to do them. We perform them subconsciously whether we really want to do them or not. While this can be a blessing sometimes (if our habits are good ones), it can also be a really big problem (if our habits are bad).

Consequently, most people have no idea their habits are controlling their lives. Most people know they have a few habits, some good and some bad, but they assume they have control over most of their own actions. Unfortunately, these people are unaware they perform their habitual behaviors on such a subconscious level, they are basically oblivious to the fact these habits exist. Why are most people unaware of this? It's because our habits are performed automatically, repeatedly, and routinely whenever certain "triggers" alert our brains to perform them! We don't even get the chance to decide whether we will do them or not. They control us; we don't control them.

That is why in *Make That, Break That*, I am not only going to show you the power of habits in your life, but I'm also going to explain the science behind these subconscious behaviors. I'm going to explain both the benefits and the liabilities of habits and break down the biological processes that drive habit formation so you can understand both the wonders and the limitations of your own brain.

The marvelous yet mysterious human brain is capable of doing an untold number of amazing things we may never fully comprehend. When we do find ourselves in a position to unravel these mysteries, we stand in the unique position of being able to reprogram the "software" within our own brains so it will prompt us to repeatedly do the kind of things we want to do instead of the kinds of things we don't want to do.

Habits are formed by the brain through design because the brain is devised in such a way as to compel us to convert routine behaviors into subconscious and repetitive actions. The brain does this to conserve mental and physical energy and to allow us as intelligent human beings to do more than one thing at the same time. It is a survival technique, and it is both a blessing and a curse.

Consequently, because habits are formed by the brain and because the brain's functions in this regard are well understood, we humans now stand in the advantageous position of being able to choose the habits that will help us succeed in life by utilizing the natural processes of the brain to create them. Therefore, habit building becomes a skill that can be learned, not a gift that is reserved for certain people. It is a tactic that can be replicated over and over again to produce beneficial habits while "overwriting" unwanted ones.

Like all good things, the brain's power to create habitual behaviors can be a two-edged sword, because the same brain that formulates habits that can help us also formulates habits that can hurt us. The brain can take actions and behaviors that we really don't want to do and transform those unwanted actions into strongly imbedded and hard-to-change behaviors that can make our lives difficult and follow us around like a shadow everyday of our lives.

In the pages that follow, I want to do more than just give you the science behind habit formation. I want to help you think about and identify those habits that are negatively affecting your life. I want you to become aware of the entrenched, subconscious, and repetitive behaviors that are adversely affecting your health, your relationships, your productivity, your forward progress, and perhaps even your reputation so you can use the knowledge you gain about brain activity in order to "overwrite" these adverse habitual behaviors.

In addition, I want you to become equally capable of recognizing the positive habits you have developed over the course of your life, because I want you to be able to see in yourself the beneficial behaviors the habit-formation process has locked into your patterns of action. I want you to see how your good habits were formed and reinforced through a step-by-step process that made them virtually permanent so you can duplicate that process to form other good habits.

I want to take you on this journey of discovery because I want you to begin to see the subconscious behaviors in your life that are restricting you and advancing you. I want you to understand the unseen processes that have given rise to both your good and bad behaviors so you will be in a position to do two things: to recognize your good habits so you can nurture them and your bad habits so you can change them, and to understand the tactical steps you can take to duplicate the natural processes of your brain in order to create the specific habits you want and eliminate the habits you don't want.

That's our challenge in the pages that follow. I learned the things I will be sharing with you in this book many years ago, and I have used this information and these strategies countless times in my own life. You see, I understand you can never rise above your habits, so I have made it my habit to learn where habits come from, how they operate virtually unseen in our lives, how they work, and how they can be changed.

Now I want to share that information—both the information I have gleaned through study and the information I have gathered through my own personal experiences of habit formation and modification—to help you become everything God created you to be.

I want you to be able to make your most desired behaviors habitual so you can perform them consistently without even thinking about what you are doing. I want you to be able to break off the shackles of those defeating habits that are keeping you from attaining the level of excellence you want for your own life. I want you to be able to do these things because I want you to do more than merely exist. I want you to live, and I want you to live to the fullest. When you can command the habits that command your life, that goal will be possible. You will be able to do the things you need to achieve in order to get to the milestones in life you want to reach. You will be able to do those things because you will have the kinds of habits that will empower you along the way.

CHAPTER 1

MAKE OR BREAK

The chains of habit are too weak to be felt until
they are too strong to be broken.
Samuel Johnson

LIKE MANY EUROPEAN EMIGRANTS WHO WERE making their way to America in the mid-1800s, George Boldt disembarked his ship in New York Harbor in search of a better life. With very little money in his pocket and big hopes in his heart, the only employment George could find was a job as a dishwasher at the Merchants' Exchange Hotel.

During the initial months and years that George spent in the United States, he changed jobs frequently in search of better pay. Nevertheless, hotel kitchens seemed to be George's destiny in the New World. With his limited experience and inadequate education, he simply could not climb his way up the professional ladder, and he had no capital to launch his own business.

Facing an unfulfilling future, George made a decision that would change the rest of his life and set in motion a series of events that would propel him toward his dreams. While still working in a hotel kitchen, he decided that he was going to develop some new habits. He was going to develop the habit of learning everything he could possibly learn about the hotel business, and he was going to develop the habit of learning to serve the customers at his hotel with as much expertise as possible.

As a result of his newfound direction, George began to make a name for himself, and he started building credibility with the management of the hotel where he worked. In due season, George was promoted. He worked his way up from dishwasher to a cashier's position, where his industriousness and attention to service made such an impression on the hotel's owner that George was asked to manage a small 24-room hotel in Philadelphia.

Even though George was grateful for the promotion, he was still far from content. George wanted to manage a "grand" hotel, not just a modest sleepover for passersby, and he wanted to manage his own hotel. Therefore, as the months and years passed by, George saved his money until he could afford to buy that small hotel, and then he turned it into a much larger facility that eventually became known as the Bellevue-Stratford, the most prominent hotel in Philadelphia at the time.

As George's reputation grew along with his hotel, he never forgot the habits he nurtured as a young man, habits that still served him as he approached middle age. George still wanted to learn more about the hotel business, and he was still consumed with a desire to put customers first by handling their requests quickly and courteously and with as much professionalism as possible.

One night, however, George's commitment to these ambitious goals was severely tested. A rather sophisticated gentleman from New York came into the Bellevue-Stratford with his wife in search of a room for the night. It seems that the couple had been traveling from one hotel to another in the driving rain in search of a vacancy. But, because two conventions were being held in Philadelphia that week, there were no available rooms anywhere in the city.

When the man and his wife learned from the hotel clerk that George's hotel was filled to capacity as well, they covered their heads and prepared to go back into the rain to continue their search for a room. Overhearing their conversation with the clerk, George approached the couple and insisted that they stay in his private suite instead.

"We could not possibly accept your kind offer," the man said.

However, George insisted. He would find somewhere for his wife and children to sleep that night while he worked the overnight shift, and he would make his personal suite available to the man and woman from New York. Besides, he knew they would be leaving early the next morning. So, after some further prodding by George, the traveling couple gathered their luggage and settled into the owner's private suite for the night, rising the next morning to make their way back home.

As the couple prepared to leave, they made a point of expressing their gratitude to George. He had been so kind to them and so responsive to their needs. They paid their bill as any hotel guests would do, and they gave George a rather sizeable tip. The man also told George that one day he was going to build a magnificent hotel of his own. "And when I do," the man said, "I want you to manage it."

Obviously, George was touched by the man's thoughtful remark, but he just smiled, regarding the comment as nothing more than a polite gesture from a grateful customer. Nevertheless, as the months passed by, George and the man from New York stayed in touch and actually became good friends.

Then, two years after that rainy night in Philadelphia, George received a letter from his friend, inviting him to come to New York to discuss an important business opportunity. George made the short trip from the City of Brotherly Love to the Big Apple, where he met with his friend, William Waldorf Astor, who was one of the wealthiest men in

America. During that meeting, Astor took George to the corner of Fifth Avenue and Thirty-Fourth Street to show him the brand new hotel he was building in the heart of Manhattan.

"I want you to manage this hotel for me," William told George. "I want you to move here and make this hotel the most remarkable hotel in the world."

George became the first manager of the renowned Waldorf Hotel in New York City. Four years later, William's cousin, John Jacob Astor IV, built the Astor Hotel next to the Waldorf, and the two hotels merged under George's management, becoming the famed Waldorf-Astoria Hotel.

As the years passed by, George Boldt became a hotelier in his own right and a self-made millionaire, as well as the proprietor of the Waldorf-Astoria, which he leased from the two Astor cousins. He also became a pioneer in many aspects of luxury hotel service. But George's rise to fame and his life of success could all be traced back to that pivotal moment in his early life when he refused to curse his circumstances and decided instead to change some things within himself. When George decided that he was going to develop habits that would set him apart from those around him, he was well on his way to greatness.

You will never rise above your habits, and your habits can make or break you. Your habits will dictate whether you succeed or fail in your relationships, your finances, and all your personal pursuits. They will determine the outcome of your educational endeavors, your professional ventures, and all your efforts to stay healthy and strong. So, if you want to be happy, if you want to be content, if you want to be fulfilled and balanced and pleased with yourself and with life, you need to develop a healthy array of habits because your success depends on your ability to display behaviors that set you apart from the crowd and propel you forward in whatever you choose to do.

In fact, psychologists tell us that up to 90 percent of our behavior is habitual. Each day, from the time we get up in the morning until the time we collapse in the bed at night, we do hundreds of things the same way we did them the day before. And tomorrow, we will do them the same way we did them today. Unless something unusual occurs to disrupt our normal routines, we will continue to shower the same way we have showered in the past, dress the same way, eat the same way, and brush our teeth the same way we have brushed them for as long as we can remember. Additionally, unless a person makes a deliberate effort to do something out of the ordinary, that person will hang his keys on the same hook in the utility room where he has hung them for the past 15 years, park his car in the same spot at the grocery store where he has parked since he first learned to drive, eat his lunch at the same restaurant where he has eaten since he started his job, and sit in the same seat at church this Sunday morning that he has occupied since the day he was old enough to read the words in the hymnal.

LOCKED IN "AUTOMATIC"

The good news, of course, is that our habits set us free from the responsibility of remembering how to do the vast number of routine things we must do each day just to get by. Habits liberate our minds from the strain of trying to recall thousands of details about hundreds of procedures we must do over and over simply to maintain ourselves in this demanding world.

A great example of the beneficial aspects of habits can be seen in the way that most of us eat our breakfasts. Most of us eat breakfast at home, and we eat it quickly because we tend to be in a hurry to get to school or to work. But, if you are like most people, you go through the breakfast routine without ever thinking about the things you are doing. You reach for the cereal, and you know exactly where to find it. You grab the milk out of the refrigerator, and it's always on the top shelf. With a bowl of flakes in one hand and a milk carton in the other, you nudge the refrigerator door with a swipe of your right elbow, and the force of that effort is just strong enough to close the refrigerator door, but not so strong that it causes the kitchen walls to shake. And you do all this while forcefully reminding your children about the tasks they need to complete when they arrive home from school that afternoon. Then you sit down to read the paper or watch the morning news, and you eat your cereal, refill the bowl, eat some more cereal, and finish your sugary feast at precisely the moment when you need to start heading out the door, never having glanced at a clock.

However, if you were at a hotel in Memphis or if you were visiting your elderly aunt in Apalachicola, things would be a lot different. At your aunt's house, everything would be unfamiliar to you. You wouldn't know where to find the cereal. You wouldn't know where to find the milk. You wouldn't know about the problem with the refrigerator door, and you would have to work a lot harder and focus a lot more closely just to navigate your way around the kitchen. At a strange hotel, things would be just as difficult. Even a simple shower would be taxing, because you would have to use your conscious mind to figure out how to make the water hotter or colder. And you certainly could not carry on a meaningful conversation while trying to figure out how to change the channels on the television.

Because of the force of habit, our bodies function on "automatic" in a lot of different arenas of life, making it possible for our minds to focus on things that are not routine and predictable. This allows us to plan the day while brushing our teeth. This allows us to rehearse the presentation for the morning staff meeting while getting dressed. This allows us to watch a television program while making toast and poaching eggs. And, this allows us to talk to the passengers in the car while driving to work because our hands seem to remember exactly where to steer the vehicle without troubling our minds for directions.

However, since so many of our actions are habitual, the bad news is that we humans can easily find ourselves locked into a range of perpetual behaviors that can commandeer our wills, inhibit our personal

growth, and limit our efforts to advance in life. Because most human behavior is habitual, most human behavior is difficult to change.

To better understand the challenge we are facing, let's take a close look at the definition of a "habit." According to *Webster's New World Dictionary*, a habit is "an acquired pattern of action that is so automatic that it is difficult to break." Now, let that sink in for a minute. A habit is "an acquired pattern of action that is so automatic that it is difficult to break." So, first of all, a habit is acquired. That is, it is learned, accepted, and practiced. Second, a habit is automatic. That is, it is performed routinely without effort or thought. Finally, a habit is difficult to break. That is, it is addictive and becomes a fixed and almost unalterable behavior in a person's life. Let's use a couple of everyday experiences that are common to us all in order to understand the makeup of the habits that govern our lives.

THE CUE, THE BEHAVIOR, AND THE REWARD

The government of the United States is composed of three branches—the legislative, executive, and judicial branches as defined by the United States Constitution. A good novel will always have three elements—character, setting, and plot as defined by the author. Our habits have three components, as well, components that are defined by a person's temperament and environment. So, while the three branches of the federal government are designed to make our country more enduring and while the three elements of a good novel are designed to make the story more compelling, the three components

of a habit are designed to make that habit a more permanent fixture in a person's life. The three components of a habit—the components that make that habit automatic and addictive—are the cue, the behavior, and the reward.

A habit is always triggered by a "cue." In other words, there is always something that ignites a particular habitual behavior. This can be just about any piece of data that the mind stores away and that the brain associates with the behavior. A cue—whatever it may be—will automatically cause the behavior that is linked to it to resurface.

According to Habitica, the company that created the popular online game designed to help people form beneficial habits, cues typically fall into five categories. There are cues that result from location, cues that are associated with the time of day, cues that are generated by other people, cues that are the outgrowth of a particular emotional state, and cues that are the result of an immediately preceding action.

For instance, some people tend to get a craving for chocolate or for a salty snack around the same time each day. Without even realizing what is happening, some of us get uncontrollable urges to chow down on fattening foods at precisely four o'clock every afternoon or 30 minutes before bedtime each night. We seem preprogrammed to eat certain things at certain times.

Other people get a craving for a hot cup of coffee every time they smell the wonderful aroma of java coming from the office next door.

The fragrance may be so slight and the odor so subtle that it is barely noticeable. Yet many of us are so stirred by the various impressions made upon our senses that we tend to develop subconscious responses to these stimuli without even realizing what is happening.

Many people start craving donuts whenever they see a Dunkin' Donuts sign, never making a conscious connection between the craving and the visual stimulus. Some of us get an inkling to call our parents every time we pass an elementary school because something about that school reminds us of a pleasant memory from childhood.

A cue can be just about anything that triggers a habitual response. Usually, these cues are things that are so familiar to us they are hidden in plain sight. So, although they are common and recognizable, these cues have an uncommon ability to trigger a response from us, usually without our willful consent. It is possible, consequently, for a person to live his entire life without ever realizing the connection between an action that has become habitual and the cue that stimulates that action.

Once the cue has been activated, it produces a very real and very predictable "behavior." It produces a behavior that is the heart and soul of the habit in question. The repetitive and automatic responses that result from the cues that activate them are either the blessings that make our lives better (like brushing our teeth before bed) or the curses that make our lives problematic (like biting our fingernails or grinding our teeth). Therefore, the behavior is the visible part of a habit, the part that other people notice even though we usually don't.

After the behavior is manifested, an immediate "reward" follows, and this reward is the thing that makes the behavior permanent. A cue may trigger a behavior, but the ensuing reward will actually make that behavior irresistible. The reward component of a habit, therefore, is the driving motivation behind the whole process. It is, as Habitica explains, "the reason the brain decides the previous steps are worth remembering for the future."

The rewards of a habit provide positive reinforcement for the behavior and positive motivation for a person to repeat the behavior that is the product of a particular habit. If the habitual behavior tends to produce a physical reward (like the satisfying taste of chocolate) or an emotional reward (like the ego-building stimulation of a compliment), the person who does the behavior will subconsciously connect the behavior with the reward and will repeatedly perform the required action in order to produce the reward he craves.

What kinds of rewards do habits tend to produce? Most highly addictive behaviors produce emotional rewards like euphoria or personal satisfaction. Other addictive behaviors produce physical or sensual rewards like an enjoyable aftertaste or a pleasurable sensation. Still other habitual behaviors will produce social rewards like acceptance or admiration or tangible rewards like money.

Most of the time, these rewards are invisible and imperceptible, but they can sometimes be obvious, too. In fact, the reason we find ourselves trapped in our habits—both our good habits and our bad ones—is because every habit produces some type of positive feeling or another physical or psychological incentive that keeps the process going. This is what forms the "habit loop" in a person's life, a loop that is initially triggered by a conscious goal, but which, over time, becomes less deliberate and more automatic. In reality, habits are so addictive and this loop is so strong, people who develop total amnesia are still capable of acting out their old habits even though they can't remember why they do.

THE POSITIVE ASPECT OF HABITS

As I have explained, a specific cue gives rise to a specific action, and that action produces a specific reward. This is what causes the brain (particularly the subconscious processes of the brain) to create and maintain the habits that we either relish or despise.

This means, of course, that people do not develop their habits by accident. They develop habits because of the rewards those habits give them: rewards that can be conscious or unconscious in nature; rewards that can be physical, mental, emotional, or financial in their design. Consequently, as Examined Existence explains it, "runners love running because they crave the 'runners high,' alcoholics crave alcohol because they crave the release it gives them, and gamblers crave the feeling of winning money." In order for a habit to be a real habit, your brain has to "crave" it. But before your brain can crave it, you have to "acquire" it. Your brain has to make the connection between the cue and the behavior, it has to make the connection between the behavior and the reward, and you have to agree to participate in the process—a process that will eventually become involuntary after repeated acceptance of the behavior, negating your ability to choose.

This is not necessarily a bad thing. It can actually be a good thing because God made us with this ability to function on cruise control. In her article, "Hacking Habits: How To Make New Behaviors Last For Good," Jocelyn Glei explains, "Habits are the brain's own internal productivity drivers. Constantly striving for more efficiency, the brain quickly transforms as many tasks and behaviors as possible into habits so we can do them without thinking, thus freeing up more brainpower to tackle new challenges."

"When we first engage in a new task," Glei explains, "our brains are working hard—processing tons of new information as we find our way. But as soon as we understand how a task works, the behavior starts becoming automatic and the mental activity required to do the task decreases dramatically." This is God's design for us, so our limited mental and physical resources can handle an increased load of responsibility, and we can achieve all our desired purposes in a complex and demanding world.

Unfortunately, the word *habit* usually has a negative connotation because most of us pay little attention to the beneficial habits in our lives. Our beneficial habits serve us well and do their good work with excellence, so they tend to remain hidden from our view. Our harmful habits cause us a lot of pain and embarrassment, so we pay close attention to those habits when we finally become aware of them, and we learn to despise the control they have over us, as well as the stigma that is attached to them. After all, everyone knows that it is hard to break a "smoking habit" or a "drug habit," and nobody wants to be labeled a "habitual offender."

Most people, therefore, think negative thoughts when they are forced to consider their habits, even though a habit can be a good thing as easily as it can be bad. In fact, a habit is a lot like the money you carry in your wallet or purse. The money doesn't care how you use it. You can use your money to do good things for yourself and others, or you can use your money to do bad things. You can use money to build a hospital for children, or you can use money to build a meth lab in an inner-city neighborhood. The money doesn't care how you use it, and a habit doesn't care how you use it either. You can create a habit of drinking yourself into a blind stupor every weekend, or you can create a habit of drinking ten glasses of water each day. It's how you choose to use your money that counts, and it's how you choose to use your natural tendency for developing habits that matters in the end.

So, we have as many good habits as bad ones. We have as many beneficial habits as harmful ones. Habits, though persistent, don't have to be unpleasant, and they don't have to be damaging. The right kinds of habits can actually improve our lives and contribute to our health and happiness. Though we rarely think about our good habits because we aren't forced to deal with the problems they create, good habits can be developed just as easily as bad habits and can become just as permanent in our lives as any of their annoying counterparts.

Just think about it! When you are stressed, what do you tend to do? Do you tend to chow down on a quart of cookie dough ice cream at 11 p.m., or do you tend to go upstairs to your workout area to spend some time on your StairMaster? The ice cream will obviously produce negative results over time, but taking out your frustrations on a piece of exercise equipment is just as much a "habit" as gorging yourself on frozen cholesterol.

When you are bored, do you tend to check your Facebook page every hour, or do you tend to read a good book? We may never attribute our success to all the reading we have done over the course of the years or to the relationships we have slowly nurtured, but we can certainly connect all those Facebook hours to our inability to function when we are away from our phones and computers.

THE POTENTIAL OF THE HABITUAL NATURE

When it comes to good and bad habits, it doesn't take a rocket scientist to figure out how our habits can affect our lives. It doesn't take a Nobel Prize winner to figure out that, while bad habits can lead to problems, good habits can lead to success. In fact, I have written a book that validates this hopeful news. In *12 Traits of the Greats*, I describe the common attributes of some of history's greatest people, and I share insights on how my readers can nurture some of the same positive habits in their lives that these giants of industry and government exhibited in theirs—habits that can set them apart from the masses and help them escape a life of mediocrity. I have spent years analyzing the lives of some of the world's most successful men and women. I document in my book the mannerisms that propelled these people to greatness because the outcome of a person's life is linked to the repetitive behaviors that he (or she) exhibits, and I want others to learn from these great people the behaviors that can contribute to their own success.

J. Paul Getty is one of the great success stories of American history, and he said, "The individual who wants to reach the top in business must appreciate the might of the force of habit and must understand that practices are what create habits. He must be quick to break those habits that can break him and hasten to adopt those practices that will become the habits that help him achieve the success he desires." And Jenny Craig, co-founder of the weight-management company that bears her name, said, "It's not what you do once in a while, it's what you do day in and day out that makes the difference."

We must learn to appreciate the potential that is inherent in our habitual nature. We must learn to fear that potential, as well, because the tree that leans as it grows will find it increasingly difficult to change its slant as the years pass by. The farther that tree leans, the more susceptible it will become to the wind and the rain. It is a fact that it is easier to help a tree grow straight than it is to straighten a crooked tree once it has grown, and it is easier to develop a new habit than it is to break an old one that is deeply rooted in one's life.

Since your habits will make or break you, the choice is up to you. They will give you an edge in life by equipping you to do great things with limited effort, or they will inhibit your life by weighing you down with burdens you weren't designed to carry and sorrows you weren't created to bear. If you want your habits to serve you instead of control you, you must develop some healthy habits in your life, habits that can produce good things for you now and great things for you in the future. You must learn to break the power of those unwanted habits that limit your life and bring you pain. In the pages that follow, I will show you how to do both.

Perhaps, most importantly, you must learn to differentiate between a good habit and a bad one. Habits are a lot like seeds: They may not produce their harvest overnight, but in due season they will definitely yield the crop they are preprogrammed to yield. A good habit will eventually produce a good harvest in your life, but a bad habit will produce a harvest of failure and dearth.

So, learn to appreciate the power of a habit before you back the truck up to the driveway and pour the cement because, once the concrete dries and the wooden forms are removed, you can be stuck with what you've got for a long, long time. And what you've got is a habit.

CHAPTER 2

THE COURSE OF OUR LIVES

The law of harvest is to reap more than you sow. Sow an act, and you reap a habit. Sow a habit, and you reap a character. Sow a character, and you reap a destiny.

James Allen

I FLY A LOT. IN FACT, I SOMETIMES BELIEVE THAT I was born in an airport. If things keep going the way they're going right now, it won't be long before every stewardess, every baggage handler, and every security guard at every airport in America knows me by name. I'm in California one week, Canada the next week, Australia the following week, and back home in Florida the week after that. My work carries me around the world and to every corner of every state in this great nation.

And, if there is one thing I have learned through all my travels, it's that no journey is a straight line. To get from here to there, you have to go through some other place. For example, if I want to fly to London from my home in Orlando, I may have to travel through Chicago. If I want to fly to Tucson on Delta Airlines, I will have to go to Atlanta first. In other words, you can't get from here to there without going through some out-of-the-way places.

One's journey through life is much the same. A person can't just decide where he wants to go in life and then wake up the next morning at his chosen endpoint. He has to travel a long and winding road to get there. Almost always, he has to take that road through some uncharted territory before he lands at his chosen spot.

An individual's pursuit of his or her destiny begins with that person's feelings because, whether we realize it or not, emotions drive everything we do. Every feeling a person has will be quickly followed by a decision that he must make: How will he respond to that feeling? The decisions that a person makes in response to his own emotions are the decisions that will propel him down a pathway that is uniquely his own.

Two college roommates, for instance, want to be musicians. While their inner feelings and emotions drive both of them toward the same goal, these two friends end up parting ways and taking different paths toward their mutual calling. One of them decides to stay in school, so he can study music and then try to make the necessary connections after graduation that will allow him to make use of his degree. Meanwhile, the other student decides to drop out of school to work at an entry-level job in the music industry while honing his craft and looking for opportunities to promote himself.

If these two young men should meet again at some point in their lives, both of them may well be earning a living through music. In fact, both of them may be famous and prosperous. But, the two of them will have different stories to tell about the opposing paths they traveled to get there. They will have different stories to relate about the outcomes that their actions produced because, even though they shared a common goal in life, they made different choices about how to pursue that goal. A person's decisions determine his path. A person's decisions determine the course of his life and the outcome of his journey.

DECISIONS AND DESTINY

History turns on small hinges, and so do people's lives. Decisions—even the small, seemingly insignificant decisions we make on a daily basis—can have long-term, even eternal, consequences. Just think about it! When Noah was building the ark and when he was telling people about the judgment that would come upon the earth, those people were placed in a situation where they had to make a decision. Would they believe this zany preacher, or would they adhere to conventional wisdom and write him off as a lunatic? Obviously, they all branded Noah as a wild-eyed fanatic, and they all faced the consequences of that choice.

This is why Anthony Robbins, the motivational speaker and self-help author, can say, "More than anything else, I believe it's our decisions, not the conditions of our lives, that determine our destiny." You have the power to set the course of your own life, to plot the direction of your own life, and to write the script of your own life. Once you take a firm hold on this irrefutable yet frightening truth, you will quit making excuses for yourself, take hold of the reins of your life, and start walking the pathway toward the destiny God has for you.

But, how do your decisions determine the path that you walk? How do your everyday choices determine your destiny? Doesn't God dictate a person's destiny? Doesn't "fate" determine the outcome of a person's life? Don't the stars and planets align to write the script of an individual's life? Don't other people affect the things that we do? Don't circumstances place limitations on one's potential? Aren't all people "victims" in some sense of that word?

It is true that other factors may play a role in the storyline of a person's life, but decisions determine the final outcome of that story because decisions lead to actions. While emotion is the "fuel" that drives us to act, it is the decisions we make in response to our feelings that actually determine what we do. Then, our actions determine everything about our journeys and everything about our landings. Other things either contribute to a person's success or hinder his march to greatness, but those "other things" never write the script.

The actions we take determine the paths that we travel, and the actions we take determine the things we achieve and the places we go in life. The actions we take repeatedly, however, are the actions that will become our habits, the actions that will, for better or worse, control the courses of our lives and set us apart from others who are pursuing a similar destiny.

This is why Dr. Ben Carson, who grew up in extreme poverty, could become one of the world's leading neurosurgeons and a formidable candidate for the presidency of the United States while other children in his Detroit neighborhood became trapped in a lifestyle of drugs and crime. The actions we take, particularly the actions we take repeatedly, will determine everything about who we become, what we accomplish, and what we do or fail to do with the talents God has given to us. Ben Carson developed some admirable habits as a young child, and those habits took him in a positive direction with his life.

Consequently, we need to understand the awesome responsibility we have as human beings to make good choices and to take actions that will shape our lives in positive ways. After all, actions that are habitual become the ruts in the road that steer us in a particular direction even when we don't know that they are there.

RUTS IN THE ROAD

I have a good friend who used to go hunting in the Canadian Northlands. Each spring, he and his buddies would jump in a four-wheel-drive truck and head for the thawing countryside of Alberta, a part of the world that my friend describes as having just two seasons: winter and the Fourth of July.

Obviously, there's not a lot of traffic up there because the terrain is rugged, the land is undeveloped, and the roads are narrow and unpaved. But by July, the dirt roads have completely thawed, so the traffic tends to increase, and the tires of each passing vehicle dig a little deeper into the soggy soil, creating ruts in the roads that grow worse with each passing day.

By the end of the short summer season, these ruts can get quite deep. And, once the long winter season begins to set in, they can freeze over and become as hard as cement. I know for a fact that the frozen ruts on one of the back roads in Alberta got so deep and so hard, the Parks Canada Agency posted a sign at the entrance to the road that said this: "Driver, please choose carefully the rut you drive in; you'll be in it for the next 20 miles."

Well, our habits are a lot like these ruts. They are easy to get into, but hard to get out of. They are created as we travel through life, repeating the same actions over and over, and they grow more bothersome as they become more deeply entrenched in our psyches and more apparent to us and the people around us.

Just think about it! Don't we usually refer to our behavior of repetitive actions as "being in a rut"? That's why it is so important for us to increase our appreciation for the long-term benefits of our good habits and increase our awareness of the long-term liabilities of our bad ones. Our habits are usually with us for the duration of our earthly lives. For this reason alone, we need to develop good habits as early as possible and avoid starting bad ones whenever we can.

Because our habits are so deeply entrenched, they can actually guide the outcomes of our lives. That's not necessarily a bad thing. It can actually be a good thing because, if the bad habits you formed yesterday had the power to take you places you did not want to go, the good habits you are forming today will have the same power to take you places you do want to go in the future. So, as long as there is breath in your lungs, it's never too late to start creating the kinds of habits that will serve you well in life. A shift today in just one degree of direction can lead to a dramatic change in where your life ends up down the road.

That means that if you tend to avoid returning phone calls, you can learn to return calls within 24 hours. If you tend to stay up too late, you can learn to start getting eight hours of restful sleep each night. If you tend to eat fast food every day, you can learn to exercise daily instead. If you tend to run late for appointments, you can learn to be on time. Better yet, you can learn to arrive early and to be better prepared. You can stop spending more money than you earn and start saving 10 percent of your income. You can start reading for an hour each night before bed. You can start solving problems instead of putting them off until they become insurmountable. You can start investing some of your free time in moving toward the fulfillment of your goals instead of just talking about your dreams while doing nothing to push them forward.

We all know that a person's bad habits yield bad results (and a bad reputation). Unfortunately, bad habits don't usually reveal their intentions when we decide to embrace them. Instead, the consequences come later, after the habit is fully formed and the rut is frozen over. Fortunately, the opposite is true, as well: Good habits eventually yield good results. I think it is better to develop new habits of success than it is to wrestle with old habits of defeat. If you can start developing some better habits right now, many of your old habits will simply die from neglect.

What you feed grows, and what you starve dies. Therefore, if you can get fully enthralled with reading a good novel, you are going to stop watching so many reality television shows. And if you can get completely absorbed in learning how to turn your favorite hobby into a profitable venture, you are going to stop wasting so much of your time playing fantasy football. Bad habits and nonproductive habits will gradually be displaced by our good habits if we will take the time to nurture them.

Habits determine outcome. It's that simple. Travelers don't just end up in Houston by mistake, and successful people don't just stumble upon success in the dark. That is why lifestyle writer Casey Imafidon can say, "Success is more about routine than moments of chance." Great achievers don't achieve great things by accident, and accomplished people aren't sideswiped by greatness while they are strolling through the park alone. Getting from a low place to a high place requires some effort. It requires intentionality. It requires focused movement, deliberate industry, and lots of do-or-die effort each and every day because things don't just "happen" in life. Things are *made* to happen, and they happen as a result of our habits.

So the habits you are forming today are already determining how your future will unfold just as the habits you formed yesterday determined the kind of life you are living today. Keep doing what you are doing, therefore, and you will keep traveling down the same narrow road. Start doing something different, especially on a continual basis, and you can steer your way out of those ruts, eventually reaching a place the other travelers cannot visit—a place they can only admire from afar.

TODAY'S HABITS, TOMORROW'S RESULTS

When it comes to life, all of us want to succeed. But what is success, exactly? Obviously, the meaning of success is somewhat fluid because people want different things out of life. Generally speaking, the quality of a person's life is found in that person's achievements and relationships. So, to be successful you need to build a network of good habits that will contribute positively to these two important aspects of your life.

I am sure your belief systems will help you nurture an admirable philosophy of what constitutes success for you, and I am sure that your internal moral compass will help you prioritize your life so that these emphases get the attention they deserve. In the end, though, it's your habits that will determine whether you achieve your goals or fail at them, and whether you have the kinds of relationships that bring you satisfaction or the kinds that bring you sorrow. A philosophy of life is only a philosophy, but your habits are the things that push you toward the realization of your dreams ... or farther away from that realization.

My North Star in life is the Bible because I believe that the Bible is God's Word to us. The Bible tells me that the God who created me has a habit of being very organized. He is systematic in His approach to things, and He has established definite patterns for the physical operations of His creation. In Ecclesiastes 3:1 (NIV), for instance, God has told us, "There is a time for everything, and a season for every activity under the heavens." (v. 1, NIV).

The God who originated everything and who put everything in its place—the God who gave everything its purpose and who crafted all the components of nature—is the same God who tells me that life is designed to be orderly and that I could be much more successful if

I would accept this fact and learn to embrace habits of order in my own life.

God designed the human eye to see, for instance, and He designed the human ear to hear. He designed the heart to pump enough blood through our veins each day to fill nearly 42 oil barrels. And this is the God who tells me that there is a time for everything, a place for everything, a season for everything, and a method for everything that matters in life. There is a time to be born and a time to die, a time to tear down and a time to build up, a time to weep and a time to laugh, a time to mourn and a time to dance. My Creator, who fashioned me in His own likeness, is a God of method and organization. He is extremely systematic in all that He does, and He wants me to follow His lead. He wants me to develop habits of regularity in my own life, so I can succeed in my pursuit of the destiny He has ordained for me.

Just look at His handiwork, and you will understand what I am telling you. The Earth orbits the sun at just the right distance. If the Earth were a tiny bit closer to the sun, life as we know it would cease to exist. Additionally, if the Earth were slightly farther from the sun, life as we know it would never have thrived. The planets, the weather, the human body, and everything else we take for granted are actually the manifestations of God's orderliness and habitual nature.

Yet God's proclivity for purposeful action extends far beyond His physical creation; God's proclivity for purposeful action also pervades His approach to man's spiritual needs. The Bible tells us that

Jesus Christ was "slain from the foundation of the world" (Revelation 13:8, KJV). In other words, before the earth beneath our feet was even formed and before man was created to walk on the ground, God already had a plan in place for redeeming mankind. Since God had a plan for man before man was even created, the positive outcome of human history was already guaranteed before man drew his first breath.

God is a planner, and God has a habitual nature. We are a reflection of him. Our habitual behaviors write our history long before we actually experience that history. The things we do each day, each week, and each season of our lives are the things that shape our lives and our destinies. They can even impact eternity.

In fact, because you are made in God's image, you actually reflect God's temperament in more ways that you realize. God has programmed regularity into everything He does. A day is always 24 hours long, and a year is always 365-¼ days. You and I also operate with internal schedules, though we often fail to think about it. We eat at certain times, we sleep at certain times, and there are "seasons" to our activities that can be detected through the patterns of our actions. Per Ecclesiastes 3:1 (NIV), "There is a time for everything, and a season for every activity under the heavens." But if we don't learn to appreciate the habitual nature that God gave us and if we don't learn to harness the power of our habits for our own benefit, we are wasting our God-given opportunity to direct the course of our own lives.

With that in mind, let me ask you: What are your plans for the coming year? What are your plans for the next five years? What do you want to achieve over the next 20 years of your life? What do you want to accomplish before you die? What do you want to see your relationships become? And what are your specific plans for achieving these goals?

Once you answer these questions, you will have a gigantic head start on the rest of the human race. Nevertheless, once you answer these questions, you need to answer a few more: What habits are you going to develop to help you get there? What habits are you going to nurture that can help you succeed in your professional pursuits? What habits are you going to foster that can help you save for a rainy day? What habits are you going to acquire that can help you get the rest you need along the way? And what habits are you going to forge that can help you spend more time with the people who matter most to you?

Success is not something that will happen to you when you are older. It isn't something that will land in your lap on some date in the distant future simply because you deserve it. Success is the feeling of satisfaction that comes to us every day of our lives when we are making measurable progress toward the goals we have established for ourselves. When a person is making real progress toward a God-given goal, that person is already successful, and that person will have joy in his or her heart.

I don't believe that any goal is ever fully attained because our goals are constantly evolving as we move closer to them. Once we reach one level of accomplishment in our lives, we raise the bar and start striving for greater feats and objectives. Success, therefore, isn't a line in the sand, and it isn't a specific point on a timeline. Success is the process of moving a little farther each day, and true joy is the process of rising a little higher each day. Success is a "today" thing, not a future thing. It is the successive realization of one's God-given potential.

This means that successful people are people who are creating habits today that will lead to the results they seek tomorrow. This means that successful people are people who have organized their lives in a way that will bring them personal fulfillment at a predetermined date in the future. Successful people have the habit of doing things that failures don't want to do. They have the habit of doing things in such a way that they can reap the benefits when the right time comes.

DECIDING YOUR FUTURE

The apostle Paul wrote, "I keep on disciplining my body, making it serve me" (1 Corinthians 9:27, ISV). This great man of God understood the difficult process of developing good habits. However, like all high achievers, he also understood the necessity of nurturing habits that could bring him success. He understood that constructive habits are hard to create and that they are developed in stages.

First, a person who wants to create a new habit will have to create it through the sheer force of self-discipline, the kind of self-discipline that Paul tried to practice in his life. New behaviors—especially new behaviors that are good for us—aren't going to arise spontaneously. The behaviors that we need to forge—the behaviors that can lay the groundwork for genuine success—are behaviors we will have to instill in our lives through plain old hard work and determination. Why? Our brains aren't accustomed to processing these new behaviors and our bodies aren't accustomed to performing them.

I wish it weren't so, but the bitter truth is that nothing new is ever established in our lives without the initial jolt that comes from self-discipline. Whether it's a highly desired personal achievement, athletic excellence, virtuosity in the arts, or an outstanding performance in school or in one's chosen profession, the journey toward any worthwhile achievement can only begin with self-discipline.

"Certainly, being disciplined does not mean living a limited or a restrictive lifestyle," says Essential Life Skills, a website devoted to spreading information about personal development, "Nor does it mean giving up everything you enjoy or relinquishing fun and relaxation. But it does mean learning how to focus your mind and energies on your goals and persevere until they are accomplished. It also means cultivating a mindset whereby you are ruled by your deliberate choices rather than your emotions, bad habits, or the sway of others. Self-discipline allows you to reach your goals in a reasonable timeframe and to live a more orderly and satisfying life."

The fact that new habits must start with self-discipline is the bad news. The good news is that the habitual nature takes over after about three or four weeks. Therefore, if we can discipline ourselves to practice a new behavior for just a little while, that behavior will soon become a fixed practice in our lives. It will become a habit. Eventually, the new habit we have nurtured will become a part of who we are. It will become second nature to us, and that is the ultimate goal.

To help you grasp this concept more clearly, let me use the simple illustration of driving an automobile. When I was young and just learning to drive, I had to think about everything I was doing when I got behind the wheel of a car. Driving was hard for me because my dad taught me how to drive in an old car with a three-speed manual transmission. I struggled to learn how to coordinate the brakes with the clutch and the clutch with the gears. I couldn't allow my mind to wander for a second. I had to focus on every process, and I had to rehearse every step in my mind before putting the car in gear and pressing the accelerator. Only through pain, toil, and a great deal of correction from my father was I finally able to perform all these processes smoothly. Self-discipline was the impetus that helped me learn to drive.

Now I can drive a car cross-country and never even think about what I'm doing. In fact, I can rehearse my sermons, talk to my passengers, and plan my next book in my head while I cruise down the interstate at more than 70 miles per hour. I hardly even think about where I'm going or what I'm doing because driving has become second nature to me. It has become routine and customary. It is automatic ... literally!

I have taken a process that originally required a great deal of self-discipline, and I have turned that process into a virtual reflex by simply following the steps that successful people follow when they want to develop new habits. And in the pages ahead, I will help you learn how to do what the most successful people in the world have done to create good habits in their lives.

To close this chapter, however, and to transition to the next one, let me take you back for just a moment to my home away from home—the airport—and tell you a true story about a man and his grandson who accidentally got on the wrong flight to the wrong destination. The man had purchased airline tickets, so he could travel with his grandson from Amsterdam to Sydney, Australia, for a special family vacation. When they landed, the man and his grandson found themselves in Sydney, Nova Scotia. That's in Canada, in case you didn't know.

I have no idea when the light came on for this man and his grandson and they realized that they were on the wrong flight to the wrong continent. But I can imagine that, when that moment came, their jaws dropped, and they had a long and frustrating flight the rest of the way. Just imagine! They were probably settled comfortably into their seats, enjoying the view of the ocean below. When they realized that they were traveling west, not east, I am sure the seconds seemed like hours and the hours seemed like days until they finally landed in Canada because they were helpless to change direction until the consequences of their mistake had played themselves out and they were able to board another flight for the long trip to Australia

The downside to bad habits is that they carry us in the wrong direction, and sometimes it can take a while to correct the problems they create. Habits have predictable results just like an airplane has a predictable destination. And if we don't pay attention to the flight we are boarding, we can easily find ourselves in a terminal we really did not want to visit. Then we have to work hard and pay a penalty to get where we wanted to go in the first place.

Mike Murdoch once said, "Men do not decide their future. They decide their habits, and their habits decide their future." My recommendation to you is that you start developing good habits now, habits that can take you toward the success and achievement you were designed to enjoy. My suggestion is that you start learning useful habits and start nurturing healthy habits so you can make your way toward the destiny that is imbedded in your soul. Your habits are taking you somewhere, and they are taking you somewhere that is predictable. So instead of ignoring these entrenched behaviors and instead of lying to yourself about their dominance over your life, learn to develop habits that will serve you better, habits that will promote you, and habits that will benefit your life.

In the end, the outcome of your life will be the legacy of your life. While most people will simply allow the unconscious power of their own habits to carry them helplessly like a floating cork toward an outcome they never chose for themselves, you will have the ability to plot your own course in life. If you will cultivate habits that serve you well, you will have the ability to determine the narrative of your own remarkable story.

Just remember: To get from here to there, you have to go through some other place. Your habits will determine which route you take and the destination you ultimately achieve.

CHAPTER 3

HABITS OF THE AVERAGE AND THE ORDINARY

Winning is a habit. Unfortunately, so is losing.
Vince Lombardi

WHILE I BELIEVE THAT NEW HABITS CAN BE created, I also believe that old habits can be broken. Obviously, I don't believe that either process is easy. Habits, as I have explained, are deeply rooted in our lives. They have been seared with a hot branding iron into the critical parts of our brains, the parts that control our behavior. Habits are "automatic." They are instinctive and involuntary. They bring us comfort and a great sense of security. They meet our deepest physical and psychological needs.

Therefore, I am not going to lie to you by telling you that when you finish reading this book you will have all the skills you need to totally reprogram your life. Your habits are subconscious and compulsive, and other people can often detect them more easily than you can detect them yourself.

However, I do believe that, with the right information and the right approach, you can change some of the bad habits in your life. And I believe that the best way to do this is to create new habits that will "overwrite" the old habits that are stored in your subconscious. If a person can truly learn to enjoy an athletic activity, for example, that person will be much less inclined to spend hours on a sofa, eating potato chips and drinking massive quantities of sweet tea and soda pop.

Before we explore the kinds of habits we would like to forge in our lives, let's take a look at some habits we could stand to eliminate. Let's take a look at five habitual behaviors that are commonplace in our world, yet destructive to our lives and counterproductive to greatness and personal happiness.

LYING

In 2011, an organization called Live Science compiled a list of what they considered to be "the 10 most destructive human behaviors." And, though my list would differ slightly from theirs, I do think these people hit the nail on the head with most of the bad habits they described in their list.

For instance, the article that Live Science published on May 13 of that year mentions lying as one of the ten most destructive human behaviors, and I tend to agree with that conclusion. While Live Science placed lying in the second spot on their list of the worst human behaviors, I would probably place it at the very top of my list, because lying is so commonplace in our world.

Lying is tied to a person's self-esteem and is thus reinforced by the strong human need for significance. Whether we do it consciously or unconsciously, all of us seek self-worth. We want people to like us, we want people to approve of us, we want people to admire us, and we want to stand out from the crowd. Hence, we tend to "embellish" the truth from time to time in order to gratify these deep-seated needs. In fact, the article by Live Science mentions a research study conducted by University of Massachusetts psychologist Robert Feldman, in which he notes that 60 percent of all people lie at least one time during a teb-minute conversation.

This kind of activity can become habitual, especially when our society refuses to renounce it. When everybody does it and when everybody condones it, lying can become a programmed response that is learned indirectly from those who mold us when we are young. And, after a lot of practice, lying can become automatic.

Lying is destructive because it can ruin relationships and damage one's credibility. Lying can get out of hand, too. Over the course of a person's life, habitual lying can inflict a lot of pain on the liar as well as the people affected by his lies and can result in social rejection, professional banishment, a wounded conscience, or even criminal prosecution.

Gene Wojciechowski, a correspondent for ESPN, tells the story of Kevin Hart, a Nevada teenager who allowed his "little white lie" to get totally out of control. It seems that Kevin, who attended Fernley High School in Fernley, Nevada, was a good high school football player and had dreams of playing college football at the Division 1 level.

As Kevin's graduation approached, he started telling his friends that he was being heavily recruited by several colleges with renowned football programs. After his friends responded so positively to his good news, Kevin began to embellish his tale further and to spread it beyond his little circle of friends. Soon, Kevin's seemingly innocent deception started affecting his parents, his teachers, his coaches, his teammates, his classmates, his community, and even the Lyon County Sheriff's Department because Kevin's story became one of the biggest sports stories in the history of his school when he publicly announced that his college career had boiled down to a choice between the University of California (the Golden Bears) and the University of Oregon (the Ducks).

Eventually, however, the time came when Kevin would have to make an announcement regarding his decision. In celebration of this momentous occasion in Kevin's life and in the life of his small community, the officials at Fernley High called a special assembly of the student body and invited the local media to be present for Kevin's announcement. In front of a packed house and in front of live television cameras, this 6-foot-5-inch, 290-pound offensive guard placed two caps on the table in front of him. After a dramatic pause, he picked up the blue-and-gold cap of the University of California and put it on his head to the exuberant cheers of the crowd.

Ultimately, as you might expect, Kevin's charade was exposed. There was no scholarship. There had been no recruitment. No coaches had ever contacted Kevin to get him to play football at their respective schools. Kevin had made the whole thing up. He had told an "innocent" little lie that he didn't think would hurt anybody.

Needless to say, Kevin's search for recognition and approval ended up hurting everyone—especially Kevin, because "little white lies," like all bad habits, grow larger and larger and produce increasingly serious consequences as they mature. Everything we do leads us somewhere, but habits tend to lead us there involuntarily and without thought.

Deborah Jacobs is a writer for *Forbes*, one of the world's leading business magazines. Jacobs says that lies—even the seemingly insignificant ones—can harm us in countless ways, especially in our business pursuits. Lies can complicate our lives, they can hurt innocent people, they can shatter the trust that takes a lifetime to build, they can repel success, they can impede growth, and they can make the one who utilizes them feel bad about himself and his own potential in life.

Lying is never a good thing, but it is a frequent thing in business and in everyday life because lying is a subconscious habit for many people.

CHEATING

Most Americans will tell you that honesty is a virtue, but our society has adopted a tolerance for deception that is interesting in light of our high regard for authenticity. According to a Pew Research finding mentioned in the article by Live Science, about 20 percent of the people in the United States believe that it is acceptable to cheat on one's taxes. About 10 percent believe it is acceptable to cheat on one's spouse.

Cheating, therefore, seems to be a situational ethic. In other words, in the thinking of many Americans, the morality or immorality of cheating depends on the circumstances surrounding each act. The crazy thing is that the research further shows that the worst cheaters are those who claim to have the highest moral standards. What people profess as their guiding standards and what these people do in their everyday lives are often contrary to one another.

This fact serves only to reinforce my premise that habits are performed without the conscious involvement of the mind, and cheating is a bad habit for a lot of people. As children, we cheat on tests in school, and we appease our guilt by telling ourselves that everybody else is doing it. As teenagers, we cheat on the promises we make to our parents, and we pacify our consciences by relishing the temporary rewards that our rebellious actions produce. Then as adults, we cheat on our resumes and our expense reports, and we continue to bury the guilt by excusing our own behavior. But with these acts and others like them, we are gradually programming our minds toward a repetitive activity that will eventually produce negative consequences in our lives, and this is the blight of cheating. This is the blight of any bad habit.

Cheating, like all destructive behaviors, becomes a habit when it becomes an involuntary practice in our lives. We develop this bad habit the same way we develop all our bad habits: We do it to meet an immediate physical or emotional need. Cheating, like lying, will eventually catch up with us and negatively affect us in ways we cannot control. Cheating can lead to divorce, unemployment, and even a stint in prison. Most certainly, it can lead to a damaged reputation.

Andrei Nana, a licensed attorney and the founder of the International 100+ UltraRunning Foundation, agrees that cheating is a learned behavior. "No one just wakes up one day and starts cheating," he writes. "It starts slowly. We learn that we can get away with things, and as we do, we get greedy and we justify our actions. It's okay just this one time. Yet the more we do it, the more we become accustomed to our dishonesty. After a while, we create opportunities to cheat every time we pursue any goal. Cheating simply becomes the norm."

STEALING

Like lying and cheating, the very sound of the word *stealing* causes us to cringe. No person wants to think of himself as a liar, and no person wants to think of himself as a thief, so most of us would never do these kinds of things overtly. What we do is compromise our standards in tiny bits and pieces in the face of difficult situations in order to solve an immediate problem or gratify an immediate need. Then, the next time a similar situation arises and we are forced to choose the behavior that will best match the circumstance, we go back to that behavior that served us so well during the previous crisis, and we gradually acquire a bad habit through practice and repetition. We also learn how to excuse ourselves for our actions while we become blind to our own patterns of conduct.

That is how lying, cheating, and stealing can become bad habits even for good people. Obviously, most of us would never lie, cheat, or steal on a grand scale, and most of us would never lie, cheat, or steal in ways that are blatantly harmful to other people. But we do tend to practice these behaviors in socially acceptable ways, the ways that our society teaches us to practice them when we are young and impressionable. We take staplers and letter openers home with us from the office. We "borrow" books and never return them. We deceive our clients and our customers by telling them what we want them to hear, not what they need to know.

Again, we never think about these practices as being bad in any way because these activities are learned gradually over time, they are socially permissible, and they produce no immediate repercussions. They are habits nonetheless because they are acquired through repeated use. Stealing in particular is an acquired behavior that can rob the soul of its peace and deprive its victims of the right to use the property they have legally purchased for themselves.

Our habits can appear to be innocent as they take root in our lives. The things that we do routinely or with little thought are the things that become repetitive for us. And the things that become repetitive are the things that define who we are.

PROCRASTINATING

This one isn't on the list provided by Live Science. In fact, you won't find this destructive behavior on most of the lists of bad habits compiled for books or the internet. Nevertheless, from where I stand, I believe this is one of the worst habits I see in people's lives.

There is something deeply rooted in the human countenance that causes us to want to avoid the inevitable. We don't want to face death, we don't want to face old age, and we don't want to face April 15. My goodness, we don't even want to face Monday mornings. We seem to subconsciously convince ourselves that if we just ignore the unpleasant parts of life that we would rather avoid, those unpleasantries will somehow go away—or at least be delayed!

The truth, however, is that certain things in life are unavoidable; certain things are inevitable. Facing these things doesn't have to be torturous. Bad things aren't so bad if we will prepare ourselves for them. And bad things aren't so bad if we will just "suck it up" and "git r done." Unfortunately, most people aren't prepared for the less-than-thrilling parts of their lives, so people too often treat these things like they will never actually happen. The irony is that by failing to think about the less enjoyable things in life and by neglecting to tackle them, we actually make them worse.

I have already told you that my North Star in life is the Bible. Well, one of my favorite books in the Bible is the Book of Proverbs. Proverbs isn't like most of the rest of the Bible. There are no characters in Proverbs. There is no plot or story. Almost every sentence in the Book of Proverbs is a sentence that can stand alone. Proverbs is primarily a book of brilliant one-liners.

I like Proverbs, however, because each of these pithy little statements gives me something to think about. The wisdom that is contained in each of these tiny tidbits of knowledge can be life-changing if a person will simply believe what he reads and start putting it into practice. I say all this to let you know that the overall gist of the book is that certain behaviors are destined to produce certain results. In addition, certain things in life are inescapable, so wise is the person who takes just a little time to prepare for the eventualities of life.

Solomon, who collected or wrote the vast majority of the Proverbs, often pointed to nature as the best illustration of the themes that he offered. He liked to use plants and animals to magnify the inevitability of certain events in life and the wisdom of planning for them. Solomon used the ant, for instance, as an illustration of hard work during the planting season so there might be abundance at harvest time (see Proverbs 6:6-8). He used the eagle to illustrate the temporal nature of wealth and the need to handle wealth wisely in light of an unpredictable future (see Proverbs 23:4-5).

The point Solomon was trying to make was that, while hard work is a virtue, planning is an asset because certain things are simply inescapable. While certain things in life are inescapable, the way in which these things unfold is largely in our hands. The person who plans ahead for them will usually land "more softly" when he finally arrives, but the person who sticks his head in the sand like an ostrich, hoping these things will somehow pass him by, will often be devastated by the eventualities he chooses to ignore.

So, don't be like most people. Be exceptional! Don't be like most people. Be great! Think about the day you will have to leave this world, and plan for it. Think about the day you will have to retire, and start writing the script of your own retirement story right now. Think about the day your children will move away from home, the day you will have to give an accounting to your employer for the execution of your assigned duties, and the day you will have to explain your credit score to the bank that is considering your loan application. Certain things in life are certain, so be certain to prepare for them, and be certain to do the things you can do right now to make your day of reckoning easier. If you know you are going to have to eat a 500-pound chocolate cake, you would do better to eat one pound per day for the next 500 days than to wait until the last day and try to eat the whole thing at once.

Procrastination brings a lot of unnecessary pain to people's lives, and that pain isn't experienced in the bigger things of life only. We tend to procrastinate in the smaller things, as well. We put off mowing the grass. We put off preparing our tax returns. We put off going to the dentist. We put off dealing with rebellious attitudes in our children.

It is true that haste can make waste. To rush headlong into any situation with no plan and no strategy is to invite disaster. But most people don't have a problem with being too proactive; most people have a problem with waiting too long to deal with the unpleasantries of life. If there is one rule in life that is firmly fixed and eternally relevant, it is the rule that what you put off until tomorrow will be harder then than it is today. It will be more costly then than it is today. A leak in the roof or a tire that is slowly losing air are symptoms crying out for your attention, and they won't take care of themselves. You will have to attend to them. To do so now is far better and much less expensive than to do so at a more convenient time.

GOSSIPING

Gossiping is a learned behavior. Like all habits, gossiping becomes a repetitive activity in our lives because of the emotional needs that it meets. Human beings need to feel self-esteem, and gossiping enables us to elevate ourselves in our own eyes by lowering others through our words and thoughts. Perhaps a greater need that drives our tendency to gossip is the need for social acceptance because human beings are social creatures, and gossiping is a behavior that helps us bond with others whose approval is important to us.

Research models show that up to 65 percent of a person's "talking time" is devoted to gossiping. Apparently, we spend an inordinate amount of our time talking to one person about another person when that other person isn't present. We do this because we receive positive feedback from our own brains when we elevate ourselves above others, and we receive acceptance from other people when we share information with them that they might not know. At the same time, we rarely receive any negative feedback from our gossip. Nor do we experience any immediate consequences as a result of our words.

Sure, on occasion we may be confronted with our words by the person who was harmed by them. And on occasion we may be confronted with the indecency of our statements by somebody who knows they are false or inappropriate. Most of the time, though, our gossip produces immediate feelings of bliss and immediate bonding with the people we want to impress without any immediate blowback. For this reason, gossiping can become a habit. It can become a person's standard operating procedure in social situations, and it can become a person's subconscious reflex when he finds himself in an uncomfortable or unfamiliar environment.

There is an old Yiddish tale that has been used for centuries to teach the serious consequences of gossiping. According to the tale, there was a man in a village who had spread an enormous number of untruths about the local rabbi. One day, realizing the error of his ways and overcome by remorse, this man visited the rabbi to ask for his forgiveness.

"Rabbi, tell me how I can make amends," the confessed sinner said to the victim of his harsh words.

"Well," the rabbi sighed, "Take two pillows, go to the public square, and cut the pillows open. Wave them in the air, and then come back to see me."

Eager to gain the rabbi's pardon, the rumormonger quickly went home, got two pillows and a knife, and hastened to the square where he cut the pillows open and waved them in the air. In the brisk wind, the feathers inside the pillow scattered in a thousand different directions. After completing his assignment, the man hurried back to the rabbi's home.

"I did what you told me to do," the man reported to the rabbi.

"Good," the rabbi replied with a smile. "Now, go back to the square so you can realize how much damage you have done."

"How can I realize the damage I have done to you by going back to the square?" the man asked.

"You can understand the damage you have done," the rabbi said, "by collecting all the feathers."

Did you know that Abraham Lincoln's coffin has been exhumed 17 times since his death, primarily due to reconstruction work at the cemetery where he is buried? Did you also know that Lincoln's coffin has been opened five times, primarily due to rumors that somebody else's body was buried in his grave? Every time the former president's coffin has been opened, his remains have been there. But rumors have a powerful effect on the people who hear them. People tend to believe the reports they receive from others. This means, of course, that rumors have an equally powerful effect on the people who are targeted by them.

Rumors hurt the people who are impacted by them, and eventually, they hurt the people who circulate them. It's important to remember that gossiping isn't about the truth. It isn't about honesty or accuracy or reality. The primary motivation behind gossip is social acceptance. It's all about bonding with the people whose recognition we seek, regardless of what our words might do to those affected by them.

"When two people share a dislike of another person, (gossip) brings them closer," says Jennifer Bosson, a professor of psychology at the University of South Florida. Gossip is one of our most popular social glues. Because gossip brings immediate rewards and few serious repercussions, it is the perfect breeding ground for the creation of a bad habit.

The "ruts" of our bad habits run a lot deeper than just these five areas of concern. Habits that either detract from our lives or minimize our potential are found in almost every vestige of human behavior. In areas pertaining to physical health, interpersonal relationships, financial management, professional advancement, and even hygiene and fashion, we humans are like magnets, picking up bad habits from the day we are born until the day we die. And these bad habits can shape our lives in ways we could never imagine.

Just think about it! Do you tend to procrastinate? Is that a habit? Does it negatively affect your life? Enough said!

Let me continue:

- Do you tend to pay your bills at the last minute?
- Do you tend to arrive late for appointments?
- Do you tend to forget a person's name just seconds after being introduced?
- Do you answer the telephone during your time with your spouse?

- Do you choose work over time with your children?
- Do you eat fast food more than twice a week?

And the list goes on and on!

Most of us want to change our lives in some way. Most of us want to grow, to improve, and to expand our potential in life. Most of us want to do better today than we did yesterday, and we want to do better tomorrow than we are doing today. Change, though, can never happen and growth can never occur until a person puts his finger on the specific behaviors that he needs to change. And that can be quite difficult when it comes to our habits, since our habits hide in plain sight. They hide in the unconscious and subconscious regions of our brains, and we rarely notice them because we are blind to their presence and their power.

Nevertheless, we can change those bad habits if we can come to recognize them. We can eliminate those bad habits if we can see them for what they really are and approach them as the addictive forces they have become. We can replace habits of mediocrity with habits of greatness if we can understand what drives our habits and if we can compel ourselves to work on them slowly, one at the time. We can get rid of our destructive behaviors if we can learn better behaviors that can replace the ones that limit us.

Habits have the power to destroy us. They have the power to limit our potential and to guide us down paths that are fruitless. It is imperative, therefore, that we develop habits that are assets to our lives—not liabilities. However, what are the better behaviors we should be cultivating? What are the new habits we should be nurturing in our lives? Do we really want to exchange one repetitive behavior for another? And what do the world's most successful people think about creating positive habits?

CHAPTER 4

THE GREAT HABITS
OF GREAT PEOPLE

We are what we repeatedly do. Excellence, then, is not an act, but a habit.
Aristotle

SOMEONE ONCE SAID, "MOTIVATION IS WHAT GETS you started; habit is what keeps you going." Motivation, therefore, is usually wasted unless it can be used to develop habits that will last after the motivation is gone. Great people—the ones who have changed the world—are men and women who had incredible drive and motivation. They were men and women who were inspired by an inner vision and a lust for achievement. But the habits that these great people nurtured in their lives enabled them to keep doing great things long after their limited capabilities were exhausted and in spite of the circumstances that may have hindered them.

In fact, if you talk to some of the most successful people in the world today—scientists, inventors, researchers, writers, musicians, statesmen, and entrepreneurs—these people will tell you that they really don't have a choice regarding what they do with their lives. They seem to be preprogrammed to do what they do, and the only thing that really changes about them is how wise they become in managing their time and resources as they grow older and the clock starts to expire on their efforts.

Therefore, if you were to examine the day-to-day lives of the world's most accomplished people—past and present—you would find people who nurtured habits that encouraged productivity in their lives rather than habits that interfered with their ambitions. If Abraham Lincoln, Henry Ford, or Joseph Addison were alive today, for example, I don't think you would find them channel surfing late at night until they fell asleep in their recliners. Rather, I think you would find them reading inspirational and informative material, saving their money so they could finance their dreams, and socializing with other successful people who could serve as their mentors and guides through the maze of life. I think you would find them planning and plotting what they wanted to do with their lives, thinking and scheming about how to do it, and working and sacrificing to make it all possible. I think you would find them repetitively doing those things that would contribute to the successful pursuit of their goals while helping them avoid those things that might detract them from their pursuits. In other words, show me a successful person, and I will show you someone who did things that "losers" don't want to do.

All the "greats" in human history—the great leaders, the great athletes, the great parents, and the great drivers of social and political change—have been men and women with desirable habits that they learned at an early age and nurtured as the years progressed. This doesn't mean that it's too late for the rest of us to develop some good habits, as well. It's never too late to change or to grow. But the lives of the world's most accomplished people prove that the earlier a person starts to build good habits, the better those habits can serve him and the more those habits can produce for him over the course of his life.

Success is a matter of understanding and faithfully practicing simple, specific habits that always lead to success. With this in mind, then, I would like to offer you ten such habits that you can begin to develop right now, habits that can lead you to success if you will start small and begin laying bricks, one on top of the other, until you eventually ingrain these activities into your life. In my opinion, these are the ten most important behaviors you can routinely practice in your life, the same behaviors that the world's most successful people have practiced throughout theirs.

FOCUSED LIVING

I believe that a motivated person can do just about anything he puts his mind to, but he can't do everything. Life forces us to choose. Because of our limited time and resources, we humans don't have the capacity to do everything that comes into our minds. Eventually, we must decide between the Cajun chicken pasta and the baby back ribs with homestyle fries.

This reality doesn't confront us in restaurants alone; it confronts us in every facet of our existence. When it comes to his life, a young man can either work to become a doctor or he can work to become a professional baseball player, but he cannot do both. When it comes to her monthly budget, a young professional woman can either double-up on her mortgage payments or she can set aside some cash for that Mediterranean cruise she has always wanted to take, but she cannot do both. And when it comes to all those precious moments that somehow slip through his fingers, a first-time father can either go into the office to complete that inventory report his boss is so anxious for him to finish or he can spend Saturday afternoon at the beach with his three-year-old daughter. But he cannot do both.

Life forces us to choose because no person has the time to seize every opportunity that arises, and no person has the resources to fulfill every dream his heart can devise. Sooner or later, life will compel us to pull the boundary lines in a little tighter and focus our sights on the precise targets we want to hit.

Great people, therefore, have habits that keep them on track. Their hearts are glued to those few things that matter most to them, and their minds are constantly planning how they can be more efficient in the pursuit of their goals. Consequently, their bodies seem to run on "automatic" as their habits carry them toward their objectives. And these habits help them shut out anything that might interfere with the dreams they pursue.

What is important to you? Is your wife more important than your golf game? If so, then your habits will show it. She will be your favorite partner on the course. And if she doesn't play golf, time with her will trump any tee time you may have planned. Are your children more important than your work? If so, then your habits will prove it. A special occasion with your kids will be a time when phone calls are routed to voicemail and the demands of life are placed on hold.

If either of those is an area in your life where your habits defeat you, then start learning some new habits today, one at the time. For example, if your family is important to you, start taking the whole clan to breakfast on Saturday mornings, and leave all the electronic gadgets at home. If you do this regularly enough, everyone in the house will start looking forward to this weekly event and planning their schedules around it. All of you will eventually form a new habit that is destined to become a family tradition for generations to come.

Do you have a dream of opening your own business? Then find some time that you usually waste—like Tuesday nights after work—and start devoting that time to doing some research into the type of business you want to pursue. If you do this long enough, you will find that one thing leads to another, and every idea you uncover prompts you to take another tiny step toward the fulfillment of your dream. In time, you will actually start making some real progress toward your goal instead of just talking about the things you hope to do "someday."

You can't do everything, and you can't be everywhere. Decide who you are and where you are going with your life because the people who never answer these two questions are the people who never really live. Until you finally stand at an intersection and make a commitment regarding which way you want to go, you won't go anywhere. You'll just stand there and talk about the places you would like to visit. When you finally eliminate all the other options and choose the path you want to travel, things will start happening in your life. You will leave behind all those lesser possibilities, and you will nurture habits of behavior, association, time management, and money management that will propel you toward your destiny.

When all is said and done, I hope you choose your career over your hobbies. When all is said and done, I hope you choose your family over your career. And when all is said and done, I hope you choose God over all else. The good news, however, is that you get to choose. You get to choose who you want to be; you get to choose where you want to go. But unless you learn to focus, you won't get to choose anything because others will make those choices for you. It's your ability to focus that will enable you to write the script of your own life.

The father left his son to cry his fill of tears, and he went to visit the optimistic twin. When the father opened the door, he found his son dancing and singing in the pile of manure.

"Why are you so happy?" the father asked. "It stinks in here."

"This is the best present ever," his son replied. "There has to be a pony in here somewhere."

Psychologist Martin Seligman, in his book, *Learned Optimism: How To Change Your Mind and Your life*, concludes, "The defining characteristic of pessimists is that they tend to believe bad events will last a long time, will undermine everything they do, and are their own fault. The optimists, who are confronted with the same hard knocks of this world, think about misfortune in the opposite way. They tend to believe defeat is just a temporary setback, that its causes are confined to this one case. The optimists believe defeat is not their fault: Circumstances, bad luck, or other people brought it about. Such people are unfazed by defeat. Confronted by a bad situation, they perceive it as a challenge and try harder."

Clearly, attitude is a choice. It is not something that is thrust upon you by the people who are out to get you, and it is not something that is dictated to you by forces that are trying to make your life more miserable. Attitude is a lifestyle that you choose for yourself despite the things that are happening around you. A bad attitude, therefore, is a lot like a flat tire: If you don't change it, you won't get very far in this world.

However, like everything else in life, your attitude is a habit. It is a choice you have made so often, it has become your fixed and subconscious response to the world around you. While a bad attitude can destroy your health, harm your relationships, and obstruct your destiny, a good attitude can prolong your life, make your daily experiences more enjoyable, and elevate you in all your pursuits.

RESILIENCY

Peter Kramer, a psychiatrist at Brown Medical School, insists that we have it all wrong when we think that happiness is the opposite of depression. Happiness can't be the opposite of depression because happy people can often be depressed. At the same time, depressed people can be happy when things are going their way. Therefore, the opposite of depression isn't happiness; the opposite of depression is resiliency.

In life, you are going to have some experiences that will make you happy and some experiences that will make you sad. Even if you are the gloomiest human alive, things are going to happen that will make you smile. And even if you are the kind of person who laughs all day long, things are going to happen that will make you cry. The people who can bounce back from bad experiences are the people who will survive and thrive in life.

Resiliency, therefore, is like a soldier's armor or a football player's padding. Resiliency won't keep you from the inevitable battles of life or from the pains that occur when you collide with other people. Still, a habit of getting back on your feet after you've been knocked to the ground is a habit that will help you absorb the hardships that life can hurl your way.

Steve Goodier, an ordained minister and inspirational writer, says, "My scars remind me that I did indeed survive my deepest wounds. That in itself is an accomplishment. And they bring to mind something else, too. They remind me that the damage life has inflicted on me has, in many places, left me stronger and more resilient. What hurt me in the past has actually made me better equipped to face the present."

So, life is going to be unkind to you. Life will be unfair. If you are waiting for all your ducks to just line up for you, you are going to wait a long, long time. More than likely, every day will offer you some new challenge, and your life as a whole will be an endless series of ups and downs. If you can nurture a habit of bouncing back when you get knocked to the ground, your life will be a lot more rewarding than it would be otherwise.

POSITIVE ASSOCIATIONS

Jim Rohn, a renowned businessman, writer, and motivational speaker, says, "You are the average of the five people you spend the most time with." There are two reasons he is right.

First, he is right because we instinctively migrate toward people who make us comfortable. Happy people aren't going to associate with gloomy people, and positive people aren't going to associate with people who complain all the time. When we want to relax, we tend to seek out people who most closely reflect our own values and attitudes. Consequently, the people we tend to spend our time with are people who are already like us in many ways.

Second, he is right because the people with whom we spend our time are the people we will copy over time. Whether or not we realize this is happening, we will gradually adjust our speech, our attitudes, our behaviors, and even our mannerisms and our thinking to conform to the people whose company we enjoy.

This means, therefore, that you should be careful whose company you keep. If you keep the wrong kind of company or if you spend all your time with people who never motivate you to do ambitious things, you need to think about changing your associations, because your social habits will dictate the choices you make, and the choices you make will dictate the outcome of your life. The good news is that you can automatically change a lot of your habits and the direction of your life simply by changing some of the names on your social calendar.

I'm not going to pretend this will be easy. Making new friends and moving into a new social circle is about as easy as changing your accent. But you can do it if you try. You can get to know new people by attending church, by volunteering at a local charity, by joining various clubs and organizations, or even by playing bingo. Every time you meet a new person, you are destined to meet all the other people in that person's social circle too.

The goal here is to start spending less time with people who complain, people who see themselves as victims, people with little vision and motivation, and people who are content to stay where they are financially, spiritually, or professionally. Instead, you want to start spending more of your time with positive people, happy people, people with good character and admirable qualities, people with drive and motivation and a track record of success, people who have actually accomplished something with their lives, and people who have already done what you want to do.

When you start hanging out with happy people, you will become happier. When you start hanging out with people who love their spouses instead of mocking them, you will start treating your spouse better. When you start hanging out with people who save and invest instead of blowing their paychecks every weekend, you will discover ways to alter the financial landscape of your life. The people around you will influence you, and you will change in positive ways. You will develop new habits that will redirect the course of your life.

SELFLESSNESS

Michael had already served two tours of duty in Afghanistan, and while he was home in New York, his natural tendency was to continue serving. Michael's sister, Kelly, tells about her brother's sacrificial nature.

"When he was home on leave, Michael liked to catch up with his friends and family," Kelly explains. "But he also continued to serve. When Staten Island was hit by Hurricane Sandy, Michael was there to lend a helping hand with the cleanup."

Michael also served his community by coaching soccer for inner-city children, and he worked with Operation Homefront to help veterans in need. But Michael was killed in Afghanistan during his third deployment, and now his family and friends miss him terribly.

Michael's legacy, however, will always be a legacy of selflessness because Michael knew no other way to live his life. It was his nature to give his time, his talents, and his resources to those in need and to give them for the benefit of his community and his country. Michael's giving nature didn't just "happen." Michael learned this way of life by practicing it. He learned this way of life by developing habits of self-sacrifice and generosity.

How about you? Are you generous? Are you a giver? Do you regularly give money to your church or to charity? Do you routinely give your time and talents to people who need what you have to offer?

The world's most successful people practice generosity as a way of life. Bill Gates, Warren Buffett, and Mark Zuckerberg are among

America's wealthiest people, but they also are ranked first, second, and fourth among America's top givers ($2.65 billion, $2.63 billion, and $991 million respectively in 2013 according to *Forbes* magazine). They delight in pouring their resources into others and then watching those people take a step forward by using those resources as their springboard. While some would argue that these men give because they are wealthy, I would argue that they are wealthy because they give. Most accomplished people have a giving nature because they have discovered what researchers call "the helper's high," a euphoric state experienced by people who engage in charitable acts.

According to writer, speaker, and sociologist Dr. Christine Carter, "This is probably a literal 'high,' similar to a drug-induced high. The act of making a financial donation triggers the reward center in our brains that is responsible for dopamine-mediated euphoria."

In a sense, therefore, giving is a drug addiction. It is a habit of the most unshakable kind because we can become addicted to the good-feeling chemicals that our brains produce every time we perform a charitable act. Since giving is highly addictive, it is a pattern that is usually repeated. Once you experience it, you're hooked. Once you experience it several times, you're hooked forever, but like all habits and "addictions," you have to do it a few times to get hooked on it.

One of the best places to start learning the habit of giving is by spending some of your own money each week on someone else. In fact, a study published in *Science* magazine (March 21, 2008) found that spending money on other people can have a more powerful impact on your happiness than spending money on yourself.

Here's a habit that is relatively easy to cultivate. At least once a week, make a point of spending some of your money on somebody else. Take your new coworker to lunch. Pay the toll for the car behind you at the tollbooth. Call the waitress over to your table and quietly pay the tab for the two soldiers eating in the restaurant (don't forget to add a generous tip). And, if you notice your next-door neighbor working in his yard, drive to the nearest convenience store and buy him a large cup of water with crushed ice.

Not only will these things give you a great feeling inside, they will they give you a good reputation that will spread like a raging brush-fire; these kinds of gestures can actually change people's lives and change you, too. They can change you from a self-centered person to a selfless one. They can change you from a negative person to a positive one. And they can quickly become habits in your life.

TRUE INTIMACY

When people think of intimacy, they tend to think of the sexual aspects of their lives, but that's not what I'm talking about here. Intimacy is so much more than just physical. True intimacy is anything that creates a sense of closeness with another person. As *Webster's Dictionary* explains, it is "a close familiarity or friendship."

Obviously, a sexual relationship with your spouse will be a lot more rewarding if the two of you have "a close familiarity or friendship." But you don't have to have a physical relationship with a person to enjoy intimacy with that individual. Intimacy is simply the ability to share your life with another person on a deep, personal level and to do so honestly and openly. Hence, your intimate relationships should include your parents, your children, other members of your family, and your closest friends.

Successful people tend to enjoy intimacy on many levels. Successful people tend to have relationships with other people that are enduring and rewarding and that transcend the shallowness that is so common in the world today. Early in life, successful people learn that when all is said and done, life is really about one's relationships. And if those relationships are phony or hollow, then one's life is phony and hollow, too. Successful people learn the habit of developing and nurturing sincere relationships that produce genuine intimacy, and their lives are better for it.

According to Kate Bratskeir of *Science* magazine (December 27, 2013), happy and successful people have learned to appreciate the simple pleasures of life, and they have learned to enjoy life's true pleasures with the people who matter most to them. They understand that, at the end of the day, a road trip with a good friend is better than closing another deal at the office. Happy people know how to lose track of time. Though they work hard, they can get totally caught up in a family game night or a child's soccer match while postponing the demands of their lives until a more appropriate time.

Happy and successful people who do great things with their lives are the people who know how to nix the small talk in favor of deeper conversation. Although casual chitchat has its place in our lives and though it is the first step in building any relationship, successful people understand the need to dig deeper in their conversations if they intend to nurture more meaningful relationships. They understand the need to ask questions, and they understand the need to listen. They understand the need to give importance to other people by caring about the things those people say and by paying attention to the ideas they espouse.

This brings me to another important habit of highly successful people. Even in this day and age when digital communications and social media are all the rage, happy people work hard to maintain real, face-to-face contact with the people who are important to them and the people they want to get to know. We cannot habitually sink into that crater on the sofa with a laptop computer or an iPhone and hope to have any kind of genuine intimacy with the key people in our lives.

So, if you have habits that are keeping you from enjoying the truly substantive things in life, make a decision today to "overwrite" those bad habits by creating some new habits of intimacy and open communication.

THE GREAT HABITS OF GREAT PEOPLE 91

SPIRITUALITY

So much of life is repetitive. So much of life is chaotic. So many things in life are stressful and combative. It is obvious that we need time to withdraw and to nurture greater things in our hearts and minds. In fact, on at least 11 occasions, Jesus "withdrew" from the crowds and from the demands of His ministry in order to maintain His integrity and safeguard His sanity (see Matthew 15:21).

I believe that all people are created in the image of God and that all human beings will be incomplete and unfulfilled unless they nurture habits that help them connect with God on a regular basis. Daily prayer and Bible study and weekly attendance at a service of worship can help all of us keep the various components of our lives in some sort of balance and help us prioritize our lives and direct them appropriately. However, nobody does these kinds of things regularly enough to make them effective without molding them into habits that will "stick."

I had breakfast not long ago with a friend of mine who told me that he hasn't missed his morning devotional time in nearly 30 years (except on those rare occasions when he intentionally planned to skip his devotional time) because this guy developed a habit early in his life, and now he finds it practically impossible to begin his day without performing this deeply entrenched behavior.

When it comes to religion, however, we need to choose our habits wisely because sometimes we tend to bite off more than we can chew, or we tend to make promises we simply cannot keep. There will always be something in the human soul that tries to appease a God that we view as demanding or to make atonement for one's own sins and failures. And the way we do this is by making promises to God and to ourselves that are beyond our capacity to deliver. Unfortunately, when we do this, the end result is not a new habit; the end result is guilt and bondage.

So, I'm not talking about extreme commitments here. I'm not talking about vows that require 40 days of fasting or shaving your head or cutting off your own right hand. In fact, I'm not talking about making any promises at all. I'm talking about developing some simple habits that will serve you well and put a healthy emphasis on your spiritual life, which is necessary in this busy, secular-minded world.

For instance, if you want to start reading your Bible more, try making a commitment to read just one chapter each morning when you first get up. That new habit will take you five minutes or so and could become a permanent fixture in your life. It could even lead to additional time in God's Word. If it doesn't, you have at least given yourself the opportunity to read and absorb six chapters of scripture during the week. (You can skip your Bible study on Sunday morning, so you can go to church instead.)

Prayer is another habit you can start in a small way, letting it grow to become something greater. And church attendance is a practice that can serve you well in life, particularly when church becomes a fixture in your weekly routine. A small, painless, easily manageable step forward is the best way to start. Then, after you see for yourself the benefits that your new behavior can provide, growth in that area of your life will become much easier.

ORDER AND METHOD

Speaking of spiritual things, organization is one of the godliest of all virtues.

Just think about it! When God created the heavens and the earth, He arranged everything to occupy its own space and to fulfill its own purpose. He set Earth in its orbit around the sun, and He set the moon in its orbit around Earth. He established the seasons. He created the ecosystems that govern the world. He founded day and night, male and female, light and darkness.

Because we are created in God's image, we bring undue stress upon ourselves whenever we allow too much chaos to rule our daily lives. A little bit of spontaneity is a good thing, even a necessary thing, but at least 90 percent of what we do in life is routine and should be practiced routinely if we intend to be happy and healthy. For this reason, order is necessary for a successful life. Yet because of poor planning and the human tendency to postpone the inevitable, we tend to wait until the last minute to do everything. Then, we tend to do the things we do in indiscriminate ways.

Think about the holidays. Each year, you are going to go shopping to buy gifts for your friends and family members. If you are like most people, you will wait until the last possible moment to do your holiday shopping. The weekend before Christmas, you will pull a 12-hour shift at the mall, looking for just the right gift for each person on your list, finally settling for something the person will probably return.

Organized people, on the other hand, know that December 25 happens every year. They put a little money aside each week to make sure they have enough to buy the kinds of gifts people actually want. Then they will start shopping early, when the best bargains are available. In fact, one person I met actually buys two gifts every time she goes shopping for a person's birthday present. That way, all her Christmas shopping is completed in advance of the holidays.

I'm not saying you have to be "anal-retentive" about your Christmas shopping or any other activity in your life, but you should do something to make routine behaviors less stressful and more automatic. For instance, April 15 rolls around at the same time every year. Why not set up a bookkeeping system that will make that day less painful? They play the Super Bowl every year on the first Sunday of February, and you've never been able to attend that Super Bowl party you've always wanted to attend because you never call about tickets until all the tickets are gone. Why not get a calendar (or use a digital one), so you can remind yourself to buy your tickets before the playoffs even begin?

good place to start building a healthier regimen is in the privacy of your own bedroom. You need to get enough sleep. If you aren't sleeping a solid seven or eight hours each night, you don't have the basic foundation in place to support all the other changes you want to make in your life.

Many Americans stay up way too late because their minds are "hyperventilating" from all the stress in their lives, and their bodies are wired from all the coffee and soda pop they drank during the day. These people run on low batteries all day long, barely dragging through the day, mentally missing many of the things they should be absorbing. Then, when night comes, they wake up and find themselves unable to sleep. Unfortunately, these reversed patterns make exercise even more difficult because exhausted people don't want to do anything that is physically demanding. These reversed patterns make healthy eating nearly impossible as well, because tired people are inclined to binge on "comfort foods" which can create more physical problems while fueling addictive eating disorders.

In no other arena of life can I think of more bad habits that people pick up over time. Our culture, our media, and even our friends and family members teach us by word and by example to eat things that are fast and tasty and to do things that are convenient and comfortable—yet not very healthy for us. The problem is that, over time, we pay the price for these bad behaviors, and if a person wants to remain fit and wants to live a long and healthy life, that person is going to have to learn to swim against the tide of conventional wisdom and

We miss out on far too many things and put way too much pressure on ourselves by failing to plan even the simplest things we know we are going to have to do. Even *this* is a habit—a bad habit—we can change by creating some better habits of time management.

In her book, *Recharged: Eight Ways To Lift Your Spirit and Live the Ultimate Life*, my wife, Christine, writes, "If you hope to have an elevated spirit and a healthy outlook on life, you are going to need a reasonable amount of order in your life. Nothing can depress the human soul and deflate one's desire to do necessary things quite like disorder and chaos. But nothing can lift the human soul and boost one's passion for life quite like order and predictability." Christine explains how a simple thing like organizing your closet can make you feel better about yourself and your life.

Like me, Christine advises people to start organizing their lives slowly and incrementally. She knows that organization and disorganization, like so many other things in life, are the natural outgrowth of the habits we practice on a daily basis. Therefore, modifying these habits takes time. Lifestyle changes that will "stick" require tiny steps in the beginning, followed by larger steps as the new behavior becomes familiar.

As a homemaker, Christine understands the psychological importance of knowing where to find the seasonings and spices she needs to cook. She understands the relational importance of having an established dinnertime for her family each night. She understands the healthful importance of having a reliable bedtime for our son every evening. She understands the spiritual importance of monitoring the music and the programming that invade our house every day. Christine realizes that order is a pathway to success in every area of life while disorder is a fast track to chaos. And she realizes that it's our habits as individuals and as families that determine the well-being of our homes and our lives. Habits are the rails that carry us either forward or backward in life.

A HEALTHY LIFESTYLE

Most people don't understand the tremendous stress that is part of modern life. They don't understand how modern conveniences and modern foods, though helpful in many ways, can negatively affect their health. In past generations, people ate more natural foods, and the work they were required to do each day provided them with enough exercise to keep them fit. Conversely, in today's world, people must develop healthy habits if they want to live healthy lives.

In three vital areas—food, exercise, and sleep—we modern Americans need to forge some healthier habits because everything around us is designed to lure us into unhealthy behaviors. One of the healthy habits we need to nurture is the habit of "disconnecting" regularly from life.

Not only should we disconnect from our work and responsibilities as well as our everyday surroundings to do things that are fun, we also should disconnect from all the modern contraptions that make our lives easier but imprison us at the same time. Every once in a while, we just need to "unplug" and get some simple exercise.

I don't want to be too demanding here because every person I know struggles to find the time to take care of his or her health. But all of us can do something to stay in shape and keep our weight in check. The hardest physical thing that most of us do all week is open a bag of potato chips, but if we don't learn to put those chips down and take a brisk walk around the neighborhood a couple of times each week, we won't live long enough to tell our grandchildren how potato chips tasted before they were banned by the federal government.

The food that you eat and the exercise that you ignore will kill you time if you don't develop some better habits. The good news is the body is very resilient, so just a few baby steps in the right dir can yield some immediate results. The bad news is that time is your side. The longer you wait to control your eating and t your muscles, the worse the problem will become, and whe your health, nothing else will really matter to you very m

Here's a good place to start: Go outside once in a fresh air and sunshine will revive you, and the soun relax your anxious mind. In fact, sunshine is one sources of vitamin D, an essential nutrient for walking outdoors for five minutes while eatin could help you start your journey to some h

do some things differently. Fortunately, initial steps in this area can be easier than you might think and can produce some impressive results rather quickly.

A REAL LIFE, NOT A VIRTUAL ONE

Every once in a while, we should just shut down the cellphones, turn off the televisions, unplug the computers, and sit on the seashore to watch the sunset and listen to the breaking waves. Every once in a while, we should spend some time with real, breathing human beings instead of their Facebook pages or Twitter accounts. Electronics are no longer just a bad habit that we sometimes take to extremes; electronics are now the centerpiece of our lives. For crying out loud, a person can't even find his way around his own hometown anymore without a GPS, and the average American watches 28 hours of television each week. That's 1,456 hours per year—the equivalent of more than 36 workweeks of 40 hours each. We need to work hard to deliberately forge some new habits that can help us bring these electronic devices into balance in our lives.

Now please don't accuse me of being an "old fogey." I may not be a teenager, but I have always seen the value in technology. I love watching television in reasonable doses, and I was one of the earliest proponents of social media within my professional field. I see great value in instantaneous communication, and I grasp the almost limitless potential of electronics. I wish everybody would catch up with the times and take advantage of all the wonderful tools that are available to make our lives better.

At the same time, though, every magnet has a positive and a negative pole, and every technological development presents us with challenges that are equal to its benefits. Take automobiles, for example. I would much rather drive a car from Orlando to New York than to walk the whole way. But walking never killed anyone while automobiles kill more than 32,000 people each year. Hence, things that make our lives better can also make our lives worse if we don't learn to control them.

As technology becomes more and more a part of our lives, therefore, we need to develop habits that can keep these addictive devices in check. After all, we want our machines to serve us; we don't want to serve them. I try to get away from these gadgets as often as I can and spend some real facetime with the people I know and love. I have a habit of turning off my cellphone whenever I'm meeting with someone, and I encourage my son to play soccer and baseball and other things that can help him interact with real people in real situations under a bright, blue sky.

The person who spends 36 workweeks in front of a television every year could easily take just half that time and do enough reading or investigation or networking to get the dream in his heart off the ground. He (or she) could learn a new language in that amount of time or become an expert in the stock market or auto repair.

Instead, there are too many areas of our lives where we have picked up bad habits that have become chains around our necks. Unaware of what is happening to us, we have been infected with the habits of the people around us, and we have absorbed the thinking and the behaviors that are common in our society. While a few of these "automatic" behaviors may serve us well, most of them do not serve us at all. In fact, many of our routine behaviors work against us, depleting our energy, taking us down rabbit trails that lead to nowhere, and trapping us in repetitive cycles of activity that serve in the long run to defeat—not prosper—us. Unfortunately, even if you are the most determined and disciplined person alive, you wouldn't have the time or the know-how to change all the bad habits you have acquired along the way.

The good news is that you can change some of these bad habits. You would be amazed how much better your life can become almost overnight if you would start developing some healthy habits to override the destructive habits in your life. In the pages that follow, I want to show you how to do that. I want to show you how to start developing habits of success. I want to give you some simple formulas and some straightforward ideas that can actually change the quality of your life right now and set you on a path toward a completely different future.

In this chapter and the last one, I have given you a lot to think about, and I know I have picked the scabs off a lot of sore spots in your life that need to be healed. Please, don't be discouraged. Don't be overwhelmed. Just pick one area where you want to make some real changes, and let's get busy with the task at hand. In time, you will make a few more changes in other areas of your life. When you see the progress you have made, you will feel like you have overcome the world. You will feel like your life is brand new. You will feel like tomorrow is going to be a whole lot better than yesterday or today. You will feel like a success.

CHAPTER 5

THE KEYS TO IMPROVEMENT AND GROWTH

There is nothing noble in being superior to your fellow man;
true nobility is being superior to your former self.
Ernest Hemingway

IMAGINE A WORLD WITHOUT ORDER: ONE DAY THE sun rises at six o'clock; the next day it rises at 9 a.m.. August 1 is so hot you can hardly stand it; on August 2 it snows. Or imagine a society without order: Your itinerary states that the cruise ship sails at noon, but the captain decides on the morning of departure that he would rather leave at 9:30 a.m. For years, the traffic lights have worked fine at the busy intersection near your house, but the city manager chooses to scramble those signals over the weekend just so he can see what will happen.

You know as well as I do that the universe could not function without order—neither could society. We depend on order for our daily lives, and all the plants and animals depend on order, too. Earth never wanders out of its orbit, the leaves always change colors in the fall, water always freezes at zero degrees Celsius, and gravity works the same all over the world. So why do we believe that our personal lives can flourish without some sort of order and rationale?

Most people refuse to plan the simplest things in their lives. Instead, they let the opportunities that confront them each day just slip through their fingers because of their haphazard approach to things. Life, if you really think about it, is nothing more than a collection of days. Seven days make up a week, 52 weeks make up a year, and a whole lot of years make up a lifetime. So, if we tend to waste the opportunities that fall into our laps each day because of disorder, chaos, or a lack of planning, we have doomed ourselves to failure. A big bunch of discombobulated days can add up to a lousy life. However, a long series of great days can add up to a great life if we can learn to take advantage of those days by developing habits that give order to our existence.

Remember, habits are the building blocks of our lives. They are the tiny little pieces that create the whole. In the same way that millions of bricks make up a skyscraper, so hundreds of habits make up our lives. As the quality of the bricks and the masonry determine the quality of the structure, so the quality of one's habits determines the quality of one's life. The quality of one's habits also determines that person's ability to take advantage of the opportunities that present themselves each and every day.

We may not want to admit it, but the vast majority of our actions are repetitive and routine. So, if we want order in our lives, if we want continuity, if we want stability, and if we want success, we need to develop habits that will give us the kinds of days, weeks, and years that are the building blocks of a prosperous existence. The truth is that all of us have the power to make our lives what we want them to be. The key to improving ourselves is to turn our desired behaviors into habits, so they can replace the undesirable behaviors we wish we could shed.

CREATING BETTER HABITS

Let's not lie to ourselves: Bad habits are hard to break. Breaking a bad habit requires a person's total focus and some very strong motivation. Even then that person's efforts could come up short, because a habit can seem as permanent as one's DNA. "Overwriting" a bad habit with a good habit is a much easier task than trying to stop a bad habit "cold turkey." Displacing an old habit with a new one doesn't require the same kind of behavioral "surgery" that is needed to replace one routine behavior with another one.

That's why I don't intend to teach you how to break the bad habits in your life. Trying to break a bad habit is like trying to stir dry cement. It's virtually impossible. It's like climbing Mount Everest in hurricane-force winds with both ankles chained together and a dead elephant strapped to your back. If you think you can just read this book and eliminate your bad habits through the sheer force of your determined will, you're reading this book for all the wrong reasons. However, a person can definitely create some new habits, and I believe those new habits can grow in strength until they overwhelm the old habits that won't seem to change on their own. In fact, a newly developed habit that is good and beneficial can set other good habits in motion and deactivate a lot of the bad habits that plague a person's life.

Just think about it! One of the best ways to get rid of the weeds in your yard is to plant a resilient strand of grass. It would take the grass some time to grow. At first, you would have to nurture the grass, feed it, and water it. But once the grass put down roots and spread, the grass would overwhelm the weeds and choke them out. It would "depose" the weeds in your yard, saving you the time and money you would have needlessly invested in an effort to get rid of the weeds yourself.

If you should try to pull up the weeds, you would only find yourself going to bed discouraged every night. You would feel like an utter failure, and you would feel like you were spinning your wheels and getting nowhere. The weeds would continue to grow regardless of all your efforts. But, by planting the right kind of grass, you could rest comfortably at night knowing the grass was doing what you could not do through determination. By allowing a good habit that you recently formed to give birth to other small habits that will grow in number, you can eventually overwhelm the "weeds" in your yard (your bad habits) and create a beautiful, manicured life.

I think it is smarter, therefore, to create new habits—one at the time—than it is to fight the old ones. I think it is more effective to nurture profitable habits, so the unprofitable ones will just wither and die. Remember, what you feed grows, and what you starve dies. If you start devoting your time to the creation of better habits, the poor habits in your life will eventually dry up and blow away. Research supports this assertion. According to a study published in the *International Journal of Behavioral Nutrition and Physical Activity*, efforts to change one's behavior are more effective when those efforts involve an increase in a healthy behavior or the substitution of a healthy behavior for an unhealthy one. A blatant attempt to simply eliminate an unhealthy behavior is usually less effective.

Let me give you an example of what I'm talking about: Suppose you had a habit of listening to the radio while driving to work in the mornings. How difficult would it be for you to stop listening to the radio "cold turkey"? It would be pretty difficult, wouldn't it? If you were accustomed to listening to the radio in your car, the sudden onslaught of silence would be deafening, and the drive would be extremely boring. But suppose you wanted to start a new habit of reading one book each month. If that were the case, the best way to stop listening to the radio would be to start playing audio books instead. If you could develop a habit of listening to something like *12 Traits of the Greats* (available on CD) instead of those giggly morning cohosts, your base of knowledge would be expanded, and your addiction to the radio would diminish at the same time.

Here's another one: Do you tend to talk too much? Some people don't have that problem, but many of us tend to flap our tongues a lot more than we should. Like so many bad habits, this destructive behavior can interfere with a person's career and relationships, and it can lead to a lot of unnecessary embarrassment. Instead of trying to hold your tongue or count your words, which could frustrate you to death and stir up guilt every time you fail, try learning to listen more. You won't talk so much if you are listening. The problem is that a lot of outgoing people never take the time to learn how to listen. When you start listening more and trying to remember and repeat the things that people are saying to you, you will start talking less without even trying.

With this in mind, I want to devote the remainder of this book to helping you develop some better habits. And I want to show you the simple steps you can take to nurture the kinds of habits that will improve the quality of your life. Before I do that, however, let me review with you the process of how new habits are formed, because a clear understanding of the process of habit formation will be essential as you attempt to establish some better habits for yourself.

In the first chapter, I introduced you to the concepts of cue, behavior, and reward. A cue is a thought or experience that triggers a particular behavior in your life; that behavior becomes habitual when it is repeatedly rewarded in some way. Perhaps a better way to recall these stages of habit formation is to choose words that are easier to remember than "cue," "behavior," and "reward." To help you recall the process more easily, let's use words that start with the same letter. Let's start calling these stages of habit formation "reminder," "routine," and "reward."

According to James Clear, a well-known writer on the subject of behavioral psychology, all your habits will be developed according to this three-tiered process. A "reminder" will trigger the behavior or initiate the events that lead to the behavior. The "routine" is the behavior itself, the action you will take in response to the reminder. The "reward" is the benefit you will derive as a result of engaging in the behavior. Although we could use a lot of different words to describe these three processes of the "habit loop," these will always be the processes that will have to take place before a habit can be formed and fixed. And Clear, in his article entitled "How To Start New Habits That Actually Stick," uses the simple act of answering a telephone to help us understand how these three processes work in harmony to give birth to a new habit.

When the phone rings, this is the "reminder" that initiates your response. Your response (the "routine") is the activity of answering the phone. And, when you find out who is calling, that is your "reward" for responding to the reminder. If the reward is positive more often than negative, you will be inclined to repeat the behavior whenever the reminder occurs, even if your mind is occupied and you are not consciously thinking about the phone.

This means, according to Clear, that in the same way there are three fundamentals driving the creation of a subconscious habit; there are three steps a person can take to create habits intentionally.

REMINDING YOURSELF TO ACT

First of all, you can create a new habit in your life by creating an effective reminder for that habit.

It takes a lot of willpower to start a new habit. The problem with willpower is that it runs out pretty fast. Even the most determined people will lose the battle against the uphill climb to start a new habit unless those people lay a foundation for their habit that is based on something more than memory and motivation.

We humans are lazy. I don't mean that in a negative sense. I mean that in a positive sense because God created man with a natural tendency to preserve his physical strength. In the same way that animals try to preserve their energy in order to burn fewer calories and survive in the wild, we humans are engineered to preserve our physical energy, as well.

Birds don't usually fly against the wind; they conserve their energy by utilizing the wind currents. Fish don't usually swim upstream; they conserve their energy by swimming with the tide. And while dogs can run at lightning speeds, you will usually find them napping in the shade somewhere. Energy is precious for any created thing, so God designed us to take the path of least resistance unless there is a good reason to do otherwise.

This is another reason we develop habits. Habits provide us with the greatest rewards for the lowest investment of energy. Life for us humans is not terribly different from the life that animals live in the wild. It's an "eat or be eaten" world out there whether the predator is a hawk or the competitive businessman down the street.

In today's fast-paced society, therefore, we often are called upon to juggle multiple balls at once and to deal with incoming fire from a whole lot of directions at the same time. We have bills to pay, work to do, kids to raise, and a house and two cars to maintain. So we live in more of a reactionary state than a proactive one, and life is a lot like a Whac-A-Mole game. We seem to be always engaged by the "mole" that just popped his head out of the ground. We don't have time to think about all the other "moles" that are lying in wait to plague our lives.

This is precisely why God designed us with the ability to nurture habits. Once a habit is formed, we don't have to think about it anymore. We don't have to consider what we might do under certain circumstances. Our actions become instinctive and mechanical, so we perform them without contemplating them. That saves us lots of mental and physical energy.

We acquire habits quickly because of the way we are made. While this built-in penchant toward laziness usually works against us, making it easy for us to acquire bad habits, the mechanisms of the human mind can also work to our advantage if we will only harness them to improve our lives. With the God-given propensity we possess to repeat certain behaviors under specific circumstances, we can utilize the sudden burst of "energy" that comes from the determination to change our behaviors (This sudden burst of "energy" is called *will-power*!) and develop the kinds of habitual behaviors that will benefit us before that "energy" runs out.

You see, that fabulous burst of willpower that comes from the desire to change your behavior is something that will be temporary at best. It is real and it is powerful, but it won't last very long. In fact, it's not supposed to last long. Eventually, the laziness gene that is imbedded in your DNA will take over and crush your willpower. For that reason, you won't be able to maintain any new behavior for more than a few days if you rely on your willpower alone. To know this in advance is a real advantage, because, knowing that your initial motivation will be temporary but strong, you can plan in advance to use that limited time to automate your new behavior before your willpower wanes and your laziness reasserts itself.

I will have more to say about this in the pages that follow because the rest of this book is basically a manual on how to utilize that initial surge of motivation to start a new habit in your life by creating the mechanisms that will make that habit "automatic." For now, however, let me just reiterate the fact that you are doomed to fail in your efforts to create new habits unless you build those new habits on a foundation that is more enduring than your temporary resolve. What you need more than raw grit is a ready-made system that can help you almost effortlessly practice the behavior that you know you need to perform, and the starting point for that system should be one or more reminders that will prompt you to perform the action automatically. Let me give you an example.

I have a friend who is helping me with some of the editorial work on this book, and he tells me that he has never made an unscheduled trip to the grocery store in almost 20 years of marriage. He and his wife do their grocery shopping once a week—usually on Tuesday—and he refuses to make another trip to the store until the following Tuesday. Unless a hurricane blows through town or unexpected guests drop in for an extended stay (a common experience for those of us who live in Florida), he insists that he doesn't want to be running to the store every day for a gallon of milk or a loaf of bread. That is something he truly hates to do, especially in the afternoons when the rush-hour traffic is heavy or in the evenings after he has changed into his sweats and settled in for the night.

Years ago, therefore, my friend and his wife created a "backup" system in their house. When they buy any non-perishable item, they buy several cans or bottles of it, and they store the extra items in designated places throughout their house. This is their backup supply. They have backup bottles of ketchup, backup jars of pickles, and backup cartons of almond milk. Whenever my friend or his wife takes the last "backup" from the cabinet, he or she notes that item on their shopping list. And when they go to the store on Tuesday, they buy several more bottles or cartons of the product they need to replenish. That way, they never run out of salad dressing or rice or mushroom soup for cooking. My friend even has "backups" for his socks, her makeup, his golf balls, and her mouthwash.

On the surface, this might seem a bit over-the-top. And it would be over-the-top if this behavior were driven by memory, self-discipline, or a problem with hoarding. However, this system is effortless because it requires no thinking. When my friend or his wife takes the last pack of light bulbs from the bathroom pantry or the last pack of batteries from the kitchen drawer (the reminder), they make a note on their shopping list to replenish their supply (the routine). The opening of the last can or bottle or box or canister serves as their reminder to make a note of the depleted item, and this practice has saved them a thousand unnecessary trips to the store at inconvenient times (the reward). It also serves them well during a hurricane or during a buy-one-get-one-free sale, when they can really replenish their stash.

Picking the simplest, most natural, most reliable reminder for your new habit is your first step toward creating that habit. The best way, therefore, to pick the most effective reminder is to utilize something in your life that you already do without thinking.

For example, I heard a sermon recently on the importance of giving thanks to God. The scripture reference for that sermon was 1 Thessalonians 5:18 (KJV): "In everything give thanks: for this is the will of God in Christ Jesus concerning you." (KJV). If I wanted to develop a new habit of pausing at least once a day to thank the Lord for His goodness and His love, I would increase my chances of success by initially tying that new behavior to something I already do.

Every day of my life, for instance, I take a shower. So, one of the easiest ways I could nurture this new habit would be to practice it while I am in the shower. I also eat dinner every day, get dressed every day, brush my teeth every day, and go to bed every night. Therefore, if I could start connecting my new behavior to a "reminder" that is already part of my routine, that new behavior would gradually become as "automatic" as the things I already do. Eventually, I could separate my new behavior from its reminder (in this case, my shower) and simply live my life with a more grateful attitude toward God without ever calling upon my willpower to do so. Initially, however, I would need to connect the new behavior to an existing behavior in order to remind myself to follow through with my intentions.

If you want to start flossing your teeth, tie a piece of floss around your toothbrush, so you won't forget your new behavior. You already have a habit of brushing your teeth, and that little piece of floss will remind you to do what you are unaccustomed to doing. Likewise, if you want to stop leaving your cellphone at home whenever you leave the house, start placing your car keys on top of your phone when you empty your pockets at night because you can't leave the house without your keys, and you can't grab your keys without looking at your phone. If you want to start using coupons whenever you buy groceries, don't trust this new behavior to your memory. Instead, clip your coupons as soon as you receive them and staple them to your grocery list, which you grab automatically whenever you go to the store.

The first step in developing any new habit is to create a "reminder" that won't let you forget the behavior you want to hone. And the best "reminder" for any new behavior is a reminder that takes advantage of a habit you already have. When you can find a way to attach a new behavior to an existing behavior so you can remember the new behavior without thinking about it, you are well on your way to making that new behavior permanent.

YOUR INITIAL STEP FORWARD

Second, you can create a new habit in your life by choosing a habit that is easy to start.

To do this successfully, you need to understand that a habit is different from a goal. Your goals are long-range pursuits that involve the bigger picture of your life. Losing 40 pounds is a goal. Earning a master's degree in biology is a goal. A habit is a small, repetitive behavior that is performed routinely and without thought. A habit is eating a salad every day for lunch or studying your biometry after dinner each night.

A habit doesn't require discipline, it won't require any planning, and it won't demand any effort once it is established. A habit is simply one of the tiny subconscious responses you make to certain "triggers" in your environment. Nevertheless, habits are important in the pursuit of your broader goals because good habits are the tiny building blocks that help you achieve your broader goals. Likewise, bad habits compel you to do things that can drive you farther from your goals.

The distinction between a habit and a goal is important because you need to understand that a habit isn't a goal. A habit is a *behavior*, a tiny "tick" on the clock of your life. It is involuntary, not voluntary; automatic, not deliberate; uncontrollable, not controllable. And, it is specific while a goal is necessarily vague.

Think about it! Your goals by their very nature are ambiguous and abstract because goals are anchored in the future, and they are still taking shape. Nobody can foresee the details of how a goal might unfold. If you have a dream of becoming an architect, that dream is going to be a lot like a city skyline on a foggy day. You can probably see the faint outline of your destiny in the distance, but you can't see all the details of every unknown structure that protrudes above the horizon. You might also have a good idea of how you want to get to the city of your dreams, but you can't see every aspect of every twist and turn on the road that leads to your destination.

A habit, on the other hand, takes just a moment to perform. It is tangible, measurable, specific, and tremendously predictable and reliable. A goal might be to "exercise more," but a habit would be a two-mile brisk walk around your neighborhood each morning at six o'clock. A goal might be to "eat better," but a habit would be to drink water with your meals instead of soda pop. Habits are specific behaviors that you can visualize in detail and rehearse in your mind before you actually perform them while a goal is the outcome of the accumulation of a thousand little habits.

Now, you don't want to bite off more than you can chew when you are trying to develop a new habit. It's okay to dream big when you are nurturing a long-term goal, but it's better to think small when you are nurturing the habits that will get you to your goals. In addition, you don't want to fall victim to the doomed tendency to force yourself to learn a new behavior through willpower alone. Instead, you want to solidify your new behavior by starting as small as possible. You want to boil your new behavior down to its most basic component and then attach that simple action to something that will remind you to perform it until it becomes a preprogrammed reflex in your life.

For example, if you want to develop a new habit of exercising each morning before work, start with something so quick and so easy it would be impossible to fail to do it. While brushing your teeth, for instance, stretch your calf muscles in both legs and consider your exercise completed for the day. If you want to develop a habit of eating more vegetables, buy some vegetable juice instead (and a "backup" bottle of juice) and pour yourself a glass each morning when you sit down to watch the news. Once your new behavior becomes consistent, you can always increase its intensity or expand its application. At first, however, the objective is not perfection; the objective is to learn the behavior and become "addicted" to it. The objective is not a complete overhaul of your life; the objective is a new micro-behavior that will become an unavoidable fixture in your regimen.

Did you know that 92 percent of all New Year's resolutions are never realized? According to *Forbes* magazine (January 1, 2013), only 8 percent of those who make New Year's resolutions actually achieve their goals. The reason for this is that most New Year's resolutions are too complicated. People set the bar way too high, and they circumvent their chances of success because they create ambitious goals for themselves that require too much concentration and too many sacrifices for the puny rewards those actions produce.

Like I do, *Forbes* recommends that you start small and build momentum as you go. They recommend that you set a goal of a few inches for your first jump rather than a few feet. And they recommend that you postpone your efforts to set a new world record in the one-mile run until you can make it around the track without needing oxygen afterward. So, try shooting bogey before you try shooting par; try bowling 100 before you try bowling 200. Try walking around the block one time before attempting to do it 10 times, and try supporting one charitable organization before making pledges to a dozen of them.

"Many people use the New Year as an opportunity to make large bucket lists or attempt extreme makeovers," says Dan Diamond, the writer of the article in *Forbes*. "That's a nice aspiration … but the average person has so many competing priorities that this type of approach is doomed to failure. Essentially, shooting for the moon can be so psychologically daunting, you end up failing to launch in the first place."

It's more sensible to set "small, attainable goals throughout the year, rather than a singular, overwhelming goal" says psychologist Lynn Bufka. "Remember, it is not the extent of the change that matters, but rather the act of recognizing that lifestyle change is important and working toward it, one step at a time."

Once you decide what your new habit should be and once you determine the reminder you will use to prompt yourself to perform it, you need to ask yourself a very important question before you actually begin: How can I make my first effort to practice this new behavior so quick, so easy, and so simple that I cannot possibly fail to do it?

THE BIG PAYOFF

Third, you can create a new habit in your life by rewarding yourself for performing it.

Remember, the reason a habit becomes a habit is because that habit provides your brain with an emotional reward or your body with a pleasurable one. Your body and brain are wired so they won't respond to your efforts to develop new habits unless you compensate them for their efforts.

Your body and your brain function a lot like you do. They don't mind making an occasional sacrifice for the good of the "team" (better known as willpower or resolve). Generally speaking, though, your brain and your body aren't programmed to do things you won't pay them to do. We develop habits in the first place because our habits provide rewards for our bodies or our brains. This means that your body and your brain are opportunistic. They are selfish. They are capitalist pigs. So if you want them to help you launch your new venture, you will have to "pay" them for doing their part, or you can just think of it as a "bribe."

With this in mind, the least costly reward you could give yourself is simple praise or affirmation. As silly as it sounds, you could just tell yourself out loud that you did a good job that particular day. Whether the reward you give yourself is verbal, financial, or some other type of reward, make sure you provide it every time you perform the behavior—especially in the beginning. Nothing feels as good as success and nothing breeds future success quite like past success, so make sure this new behavior is something you want for yourself, not something your spouse or your friends are forcing upon you. If the behavior is indeed something you want in your life, you will find it much easier to perform that behavior consistently if you reward yourself for doing it.

"Rewards should be about the same 'size' as your habit," says Stephen Guise, author of *Mini Habits: Smaller Habits, Bigger Results*. "If you do one sit-up every day and always have a full bowl of ice cream afterwards, you might be forming the wrong habit."

So, with this in mind, Guise recommends rewards that are equivalent to the behaviors we are trying to form. He recommends things like eating a small piece of chocolate or taking a break to spend time with a person who makes you laugh, both of which are "guilt-free" rewards for performing a new behavior as required. He also recommends watching a movie at home or at the theater or taking a nap or going out to eat. Behaviors are reinforced through rewards, so Guise practices what he preaches, and he preaches what is true.

The type of reward that you attach to your new behavior is up to you. All that matters is that you reward yourself for each performance you complete and that you make the reward appropriate for the action you have executed. Small steps equal small rewards! Big steps equal big rewards! If you do this faithfully and consistently, you will gradually reprogram your subconscious so it takes over the process and makes the new behavior as automatic as breathing or blinking your eyes.

If the new behavior you are rewarding is not exactly what you had hoped it would be, don't worry about it during the initial stages of formation. As I explained earlier, you can always add to the behavior as it takes root or expand the behavior or broaden it once it has been ingrained in your life. But at first, you want to make the behavior simple to perform and easy to reward. You want to make it as much fun as possible, and you want to pay yourself well for remembering it and performing it. God gave you a slight advantage in this competition between the "you" that you want to create and the "you" that currently exists. He has given you the advantage of knowing how your brain works. But like any athlete who knows the tactics of his opponent, you need to act on your newfound knowledge as you coax your own subconscious into following the steps I have offered to you.

Obviously, this proven approach to habit formation is a basic plan that will have to be customized to fit your personality, your lifestyle, your circumstances, and the habit you want to form. This three-tiered approach, however, is almost always effective if you will take some time to plan your success before launching your assault. And yes, I said "assault." By attempting to create a new habit in your life, you will be paddling against the tide. But you can do it if you refuse the temptation to fight your own habitual nature and choose instead to "go with the flow" by making the process easy and by utilizing your own tendency to habituate simple actions that provide you with an immediate reward.

So, give some thought to how you can make your desired behaviors permanent. Give some thought to how you can make them fun. Be creative as you choose your reminders and as you come up with your rewards. Be imaginative as you determine the best ways to make your new behaviors simple and easy. In the pages that follow, I will give you a more precise formula and some practical suggestions for creating better habits in your life and for making the habits you form as permanent as the bad habits you wish you could change. Before you start, you need to determine the first new habit you want to create. Then you should give some thought to the tactics you can employ to make it last forever.

CHAPTER 6

CHANGING YOUR HABITS

*Everyone thinks of changing the world, but
no one thinks of changing himself.*
Leo Tolstoy

SCIENCE HAS FINALLY PROVEN WHAT HISTORY already reveals: Big achievers are driven by big dreams. People who do great things and build great things, people who open doors to new ideas and who lead others through those doors, are people who first had lofty goals that compelled them to do the things they did.

In fact, in a recent scientific study, researchers concluded that, to do great and noble things, a person must have an unusually high level of self-discipline. That is, he (or she) must have the ability to say "no" to himself temporarily in order to say "yes" to himself at a later date. However, the same research concluded that nobody makes these kinds of sacrifices unless that person is driven by a passion that is more important to him than the amusements or distractions that may divert him from his course.

All the great people in human history, from the great explorers to the greatest athletes, were driven by a dream to go places other people had never gone, to do things other people had never done, and to solve problems that other people deemed unsolvable. Great entrepreneurs like Henry Ford and great leaders like Winston Churchill could see in their mind's eye things that other people could not see, and they could see in their souls a pathway for accomplishing what other people considered unattainable.

Grand thinking, therefore, almost always precedes grand achievement. Vision almost always precedes accomplishment. Desire, motivation, and self-sacrifice almost always precede success. People pay the price to realize their dreams because of a burning passion that consumes them inwardly. They sacrifice and toil because of a clear mental picture that pushes them forward against all odds toward an ideal that most people could never appreciate.

Consequently, big ideas and big goals drive big achievements, and passion for one's dreams is the fuel that pushes a person to succeed. There is another component to success that I have tried to convey throughout this book also. Not only is success the product of the visualization of a goal; success is the product of the activities a person performs each day in the deliberate pursuit of that goal. While success is the result of one's goal-oriented thinking, success is also the

result of one's willingness to do the thousands of little things that are necessary to make that goal a reality. This is where habits come into play. Habits are the "little things" that add up to carry us toward the "bigger things" in life. Habits are the tiny steps that join together to create a great journey. Allow me to demonstrate.

Several years ago I became interested in the power of personal habits and in the ability of habits to either propel a person toward success or hinder that person from achieving his full potential in life. After thinking about habits for a few years and after reading a lot of material on the habitual nature of human beings, I came up with a personal approach to habit formation that I thought could make my life a lot better. After implementing my newfound knowledge with impressive results, I soon realized that I wanted to share my discovery with other people. That's when the idea for this book came into my mind as the best strategy for explaining my experiences and insights. And the more I thought about this book, the more clearly I could see it in my mind and the more clearly I could imagine the chapters I would need to write to help people understand my approach to habit formation.

Having a long-range goal to write a book, however, did little to make this book a reality. In fact, I have always been saddened by the fact that cemeteries are filled with people who had ideas for great books yet never did anything to bring those books to life. I knew I would have to do more than just think about this book in order to put it on paper and put it into the hands of the people who needed it. I knew

I would have to give some thought to the day-to-day effort I would need to put behind my dream in order to drive it to completion.

I wish I could have snapped my fingers and somehow caused this book to be published. I wish I could have rubbed a magic lamp and just handed this project off to a genie. After all, I knew the idea was a good one. Unfortunately, dreams aren't achieved by wishing or by wanting. Dreams only come to pass when we roll up our sleeves and put our hands all over those dreams by doing the hard work that is necessary to drive those dreams to fulfillment. Good ideas don't guarantee success; success comes when a good idea is followed with the hard labor that is necessary to give substance to the thought.

I decided to do a little work each day to make my book a reality, and I felt a tremendous sense of satisfaction when I was able to go to bed at night knowing that I had made progress that day in the pursuit of my goal. I did my research, I recorded my thoughts on paper, I recorded additional thoughts on tape, I enlisted people to help me whenever I encountered problems I could not solve, and I pushed this book an inch or two forward every single day. Now you are reading a book that was once nothing more than a thought in my head, a notion in my heart, and it was the work that made it happen. It was the daily routines piled one upon another and repeated with regularity and faithfulness that gave substance to my ambitious goal.

Through this lengthy process, the inspiration for my persistence came from a true story I once read about a lawyer who secretly longed to be

a best-selling author. But while my own aspirations for writing were focused on the nonfiction world, this attorney wanted to be a novelist. Unfortunately, like the rest of us, he was far too busy to pursue his dream. He worked 60 to 80 hours each week, and the little time he had left was devoted to his family, his friends, and his community. It looked like he was destined to follow the majority of the people who had come before him by allowing his dream to die with him at the end of his life.

One day this lawyer realized that, in spite of his many obligations, his dream could still come true if he would only make one simple change in his life. So, at that moment, he had a choice to make: He could keep living his life the way he was living it, or he could stop making excuses for himself and start carving out the time he needed in order to make his dream a reality.

After deciding that he was going to "bite the bullet" and do what it took to put his book on paper, this man forged a new habit of getting up two hours earlier each morning so he could work on the manuscript he had always dreamed of writing. At 5 a.m. each day, he crawled out of his warm bed, switched on his small personal computer, and pecked away at the keys while his family continued to sleep. Finally, after a lot of lonely hours and after a year of hard work, he had his first novel in hand, ready to offer to a waiting world.

When this accomplished lawyer sent his manuscript to a publisher, the publisher rejected it. Then he sent it to another publisher, and another publisher, and another and another. In fact, he sent his novel to 26 publishers before somebody finally decided to take a chance on him and put his book in print. But even then, enthusiasm for his book was underwhelming because the publisher printed only 5,000 copies, and nobody bought any of them. The book bombed big time!

Therefore, the attorney was faced with another choice, and he made the hard decision to purchase 1,000 copies of his own book in order to market them himself. With a thousand books in tow, he started visiting bookstores and libraries, and he started organizing book sign-ings and attending public events where he could make speeches and sell his books. Eventually, John Grisham's efforts paid off, because his book, *A Time to Kill*, somehow gained popularity and paved the way for a writing career that has included 30 novels and more than 275 million books sold since 1989. All because this lawyer had a dream! All because this would-be author made up his mind to develop a new habit in his life that would enable him to do something to move his dream forward instead of wallowing in his own self-pity while making excuses for himself!

HABITS FLOW FROM DESTINY

Dreams are precious things, and they are the seeds of greatness. As I said at the beginning of this chapter, all great accomplishments begin with a dream. They begin with an idea. But, in the same way that a seed lies dormant until it is placed in the soil and watered, so a dream lies dormant until it is brought to life through hard work and effort, through sacrifice and deliberate changes in one's habits.

So, with this in mind, let me ask you: What is your dream? What is your driving ambition in life? The goals you want to achieve tomorrow will dictate the things you need to do right now in order to give substance to those goals. The achievements you hope to celebrate in the future will dictate the habits you need to forge right now in order to push the seeds of those achievements up through the soil and toward the light of day.

Take the salesperson, for instance, who dreams about managing his own store. That salesperson is going to think about being a manager, and he (or she) is going to visualize what life would be like if he suddenly found himself in a management position. In response to those fantasies about the future, he is going to begin his climb to the top by imagining what it would be like if he were the manager at the store where he works right now. These mental visualizations of his dream will motivate him to pay attention to his present manager in a way the other employees never would. His dream will compel him to learn from his own manager by watching what the manager does and by thinking about the things the manager isn't doing—but should be doing.

Just think about it! The person who visualizes an inner goal is the person who will study the habits of those who are already doing what he wants to do. The salesperson in this illustration is going to devour information that can help him learn what he needs to know about owning and operating his own business. He will watch the manager of his own store and the managers of other stores, so he can learn what they do to succeed. He may even talk to some of these people about the things they do habitually to make themselves successful.

Perhaps our would-be entrepreneur observes that several successful managers get up early each morning and get to the store at least an hour before the other employees arrive. Or perhaps he notices that the managers of the most productive stores return their phone calls at set times each day. Regardless of what the success habits of the best managers may be, our up-and-coming manager will soon realize through observation and interaction that there are certain behaviors that tend to set the best managers apart. He will realize that certain behaviors make these managers stand out from a sea of ordinary people who barely "manage" to get by (pun intended).

He adopts the behaviors that he thinks will work for him, so he can start nurturing the habits he knows he will need to position himself for success. He doesn't adopt every habit he sees in others, because some of those habits won't align with his needs, his temperament, or his circumstances. He does adopt the ones he can utilize, and he works to instill those behaviors in his life.

This is why, in a perfect world, you should know your purpose before you adopt your habits. Only by knowing your destination can you forge the habits you will need to succeed in your quest. People acquire bad habits because they have no personal vision that drives them toward a specific goal. Once you know where you are going, you will better understand how to get there. You will slowly but surely plot the course, plan the steps, and obtain the skills, relationships, and resources you will need to complete your journey. You will instinctively develop the habits that help you get from here to there and from where you are to where you want to be. As you read books, take classes, and model the lives of those who have already ventured where you want to go, you will come to appreciate those repetitive behaviors that have helped your predecessors succeed, and you will adopt many of those habits for yourself while developing some of your own habits that may prove to serve you well. Your future goals, therefore, will determine your current habits, and your current habits will make possible the apprehension of your goals.

Small daily steps lead to great big achievements. Big goals without small steps will usually come to naught because the habits that drive your daily life eventually make your dreams achievable in the same way that a whole lot of tiny steps make a long journey achievable. And this is why it is important that you develop new habits in your life that can help you take the steps you need to take each day to propel your life in the direction you want to travel.

MAKING IT HAPPEN

I share all this with you because I have learned through simple observation that many dreams never come to fruition, not because the dreams are unrealistic and not because the dreamers are unqualified to achieve them. These dreams are aborted before they are hatched because the people who conceived them are incapable of giving them life. People are incapable of pushing their dreams through the birth canal. The person who lacks the daily habits that equip him to do what he is destined to do is the person who will never do what he is destined to do. His bad habits or lack of good habits won't allow him to do great things. Unfortunately, this seems to be true for the majority of the people out there.

I don't want you to be numbered in the majority. I want you to be the exception to the rule. I want you to be great and to attain every worthy goal that God has planted in your heart and mind. I want you to be able to do what you were created to do and designed by God to do with your life. Here's how you can do that: You can do that by gradually developing habits, one at a time, that will equip you to do the things you need to do each day to propel yourself toward the bigger picture of your life's purpose. The first step in doing this is to make a list of all the unproductive habits in your life that could keep you from achieving that goal.

That's right! I want you to make a list of all your bad habits, especially the ones that hinder you relationally or professionally. Maybe you tend to procrastinate. Maybe you run late paying your bills. Maybe you talk over people or you bite your fingernails in public. Whatever your faults may be, I want you to write them down. And if you are really brave, you can ask some of the people who are closest to you to help you develop your list. The key here is not to degrade yourself or to bathe yourself in guilt or self-pity; the key here is to objectively identify those subconscious patterns of behavior that are limiting your future potential. Start by noticing them and writing them down. Look for your repetitive responses to people and to the world around you, and make a note of the behaviors that you wish would go away. Spend a few days or a week or even longer watching yourself and noting those repetitive actions that you know are holding you back.

Do you put off collecting your past-due accounts? You need to note that bad habit because successful entrepreneurs are always on top of their finances. Do you tend to run late for appointments? Then you need to put that habit on your list because successful businesspeople in all fields know the negative message that their tardiness can convey.

Do you forget a person's name just moments after being introduced? Include that bad habit in your inventory because no person can feel good about you and become open to your guidance or your presentation if your behavior tells him that he is a low priority to you.

Do you answer the phone when you're spending "us time" with your spouse? If so, you just told your spouse that he or she is secondary in your life.

Do you routinely choose work over time with your children? Then unfortunately, you are destined to see the results of those choices when your children reach adolescence.

Do you eat a lot of fast food because you find it convenient when you're on the run? Then buy life insurance now while you can afford it because you won't be able to pass a physical once you reach the age of 50.

Does tax season always sneak up on you? Do you forget birthdays and anniversaries? Is your laugh too loud and obnoxious? Do you tend to inject your political beliefs into conversations with people you just met? Write these things down because these behaviors affect your relationships, and your relationships affect your life. Write these things down because these things affect your business, and your business affects your financial stability. Write these things down because these things affect your financial stability, and your financial stability affects your capacity to do what you want to do with your life. *Write these things down*, because these things affect every vestige of your life from your reputation to your expectations, from your personal significance to your legacy.

The purpose of this exercise is to explore the true nature of your life: your family life, your professional life, your spiritual life, and your social life. Through this exercise, you should be able to investigate every important aspect of your life and even to explore your health. The purpose of this exercise is to help you see yourself as other people see you because, before you can create the kinds of habits that will position you to take advantage of tomorrow's opportunities, you need a clear image of your life as it stands today. Only by developing a clear picture of your strengths and weaknesses can you ever hope to succeed in your pursuits.

Once you have taken a reasonable amount of time to identify and record your bad habits, the next thing I want you to do is to determine the good habits you would like to create in place of the bad ones. Do you want to start exercising regularly? Do you want to start contributing faithfully to your church? Do you want to start eating healthier? Do you want to start spending more time with your children or your spouse? Do you want to start saving money instead of wasting it? Do you want to start reading more and learning about subjects that interest you? Your list could be endless. If you will note the habits you think could enhance your life and then prioritize those habits on paper or in your mind, this could become a real turning point in your climb to success. This could become your "pivot point" in life.

After noting the worst habits in your life and the new habits you want to form to replace them, the final step I want you to take is to develop the "systems" that will enable you to nurture your new habits. For example, if your goal is to start going to the gym every morning before work, one system that could help you succeed in this new venture is to set your clock ahead one hour. That way, you could go to bed an hour earlier each night and get up an hour earlier each morning without stressing over the change in your schedule.

Here's another suggestion: If you happen to work in sales, instead of operating in a perpetual state of chaos and flying by the seat of your pants every time you land a hot lead, you could develop a checklist of all the processes you need to perform in order to more effectively follow up with each of your new prospects. This way, the system would be set in stone, and all your prospects would receive the same series of communications and the same contacts from you in the same order and according to the same timeline. No prospective client would ever "fall through the cracks" because of neglect. And, you could easily pinpoint over time the processes that are most effective and the processes that are wasting your time and money.

So, determine the habit you want to develop and then give some thought to the system you could employ to help you overcome the barriers that have kept you from forming that habit in the past. At this point, I don't want you to actually implement any kind of system. In the pages that follow, I am going to show you a very easy way to systematize your efforts so you can form new habits in a relatively effortless way. For now, I just want you to start thinking about a system that could make your new habit more natural and less stressful. Choose the habit you want to develop and give some thought to the system you could form that would help you solidify that new habit as an enduring part of your life. Remember, habits aren't formed in a vacuum; they are formed in a structure that creates repetitiveness for the behavior you want to forge. In the same way that a train rides on a structure of steel rails, so a habit rides on the structure of a system that makes the behavior routine. To succeed in creating a new habit, therefore, you need to be proactive by devising your own system for that habit, a system that will give you success.

Let's imagine that you want to develop the habit of finishing all your work by the end of business on Friday, so your mind can be free on the weekends for your children and your husband or wife. If so, you can't just "decide" that you are going to suddenly start finishing your work by five o'clock every Friday. You have to create the system that will make your goal possible.

How can you create a system like this? Will you develop a checklist of all the things you need to do each day to stay on track for the week? Will you spend less time chatting with your coworkers and more time filing your paperwork? Will you eat lunch in the office on Fridays to guarantee that you finish on time? Will you start delivering promised documents to your clients on Thursdays instead of Fridays, so you can avoid putting pressure on yourself at the end of the workweek?

What exactly are you going to do differently to help you succeed in your efforts to form this new habit? That is the question you need to ask yourself as you ponder the system that will help you create the repetitive behavior. Remember, success doesn't happen by accident. It happens because somebody makes it happen. And people make things happen by planning to make them happen, not by simply hoping that they will happen.

KNOWING WHERE YOU STAND

In the next chapter, I will be focusing on this third and final step in our three-step process of creating new habits. I will be sharing with you my "system" for creating new habits and making them a permanent part of your life. I will be walking you through all the practical things you can do to take advantage of your brain's habitual nature and utilize the "habit loop" that is written into your DNA.

But for now, before you start reading the next chapter and thinking about the system you will devise to help you create your own good habits, I want you to focus on the first two exercises I have given you to do. I want you to do some serious thinking about the bad habits you wish you could eliminate and the good habits you wish you could form. I want you to start making the journey to a better "you" by becoming aware of the habits that currently rule your life; then, I want you to imagine the new habits that could make your life a lot better.

Until you know where you stand, you cannot know where you're going. Until you know what you lack, you cannot know what you need. That is why it would be wise to enlist the help of others as you take a hard look at the destructive habits that rule your life, and that is why you need to spend some "alone time" as you think about the behaviors you would like to adopt instead.

But whether you do these two processes alone or with the help of others, your task between now and the next chapter is to understand how your current behaviors negatively affect your life. And by extension, this exercise should help you understand how some better habits could positively affect you, because awareness is the first step in replacing unproductive habits with productive ones, and imagination is the tool that will help you create your "system."

After all, you can't really know what you have until you take stock of it, and you can't really know what you need until you take a step back so you can focus on the bigger picture. And once you have done these things, I will help you make use of the discoveries you have made. I will help you put the systems in place that can lead to the elimination of your bad habits and the establishment of new habits that are destined to lead you to success.

CHAPTER 7

THIRTEEN WEEKS

Winners make a habit of doing the things losers don't want to do.
Lucas Remmerswaal

HAVE YOU FINISHED COMPILING YOUR LISTS? HAVE you spent some time thinking about your good habits and your bad ones? If so, I hope you have learned something about yourself and about the opportunities that await you as well as the obstacles that stand in your way.

I understand that the exercise I recommended in the last chapter has the potential for being disheartening. After all, nobody likes to see the flaws in his or her life. It is human nature to seek affirmation, not analysis. It is human nature to seek encouragement, not criticism. However, no doctor can cure what ails you unless that doctor takes a look at your condition, and the tests your doctor performs will never lie. As uncomfortable as those tests may be, they are designed to give your doctor an accurate appraisal of your present state of health. Then, having that knowledge in hand, your doctor can do some amazing things to make your life a lot better.

So, your lists were absolutely essential in your effort to build a better life. Creating them may have been a little unpleasant, just as your doctor's tests can be unpleasant, and they may have shown you some things that made you feel a bit gloomy. But those lists have provided you with a more accurate picture of the strengths and the weaknesses you possess. That knowledge will be priceless as you seek to overcome the limitations that hinder you.

Your "tests" are now over, and the time has finally come to diagnose your situation and offer a prognosis for the future. With that goal in mind, I want you to temporarily set aside the list of your negative habits. I don't want you to forget that list altogether or ignore the realities that you discovered about yourself, because obviously, now that you are aware of some of your negative traits, you want to start eliminating them from your life. However, I want you to temporarily set that list aside for two reasons.

One, I want you to begin the growth process by focusing on the positive goals ahead of you, not the problems caused in the past by the bad habits that afflict you. And two, I think you will find that, as you focus on creating some better habits for yourself, many of your old habits will simply fade away, and you won't have to grapple with them any longer. As I explained earlier, many of your bad habits will disappear like an odor in a stiff wind if you will focus instead on the positive task of creating good habits for yourself. That will take some time, but perhaps you can hold onto your list of bad habits and revisit that list from time to time, so you can see that I am telling you the truth.

At this point, I want all your attention on the list of those good habits you would like to add to your routines. If you have prioritized that list in some way, you are now ready to move into the next phase of our mission to change the course of your life. You are ready to actually start doing the work that is necessary for creating good habits for yourself.

WHERE TO START

With your list in hand, I want you to choose the first four habits you would like to establish and prioritize those habits one through four because my plan in this chapter is to give you my 13-week program for adopting a new habit and for making it a permanent fixture in your life. The idea here is to work on one new habit at a time—13 weeks for each habit—thus creating a total of four new habits during the coming year.

Just think about that! What could you accomplish in your life if you could develop four new and powerful habits over the next 12 months? What could you achieve if you could institute four new constructive habits during the coming year that are capable of taking you in the direction you want to travel? That is an amazing thought.

Therefore, I want you to set a goal for yourself of solidifying these four habits in your life over the next year (13 weeks per habit), and I want you to watch what happens as you do that by employing the plan I am about to give you. I want you to set a goal of developing and nurturing these four new behaviors, so they become repetitive and habitual and your automatic responses to the world around you. Then, not only should these new behaviors become ingrained in your response patterns over each 13-week period, but they should gradually replace some of the old habits you haven't been able to shake until now.

As you determine the four habits you want to establish over the next 12 months, you should be aware that this is the point where all our research will merge. This is the point where all the information involving the cue, the behavior, and the reward (also known as the reminder, the response, and the reward) will become applicable to you personally. This is the point where all our observations involving "systems" will really start to make sense. This is the point where I will be tying all the loose ends together so you can fully understand the dynamics of habit formation and the practical mechanisms you can employ to form new habits.

This venture should be exciting as you contemplate the possibilities. Right now, you have a list of bad habits you wish you could eliminate.

And right now, you have a list of good habits you wish you could learn. If you follow my 13-week plan, you could have four new habits a year from now that could radically change your life, and you could be free from some of your bad habits without ever trying to overcome them.

In addition, you should be encouraged by the knowledge that you don't have to stop with just four new habits. If you keep doing the things I am about to teach you, you could have 20 new habits just five years from now. Then 10 years from now, you could have 40 new habits of success. And the benefits of these new habits will start producing returns for you that will work like compound interest. The advantages derived from one new habit will help feed your efforts to start the next new habit, and the results you see in your life will produce exponential returns for you in your relationships, finances, professional pursuits, and health. They will also produce returns for you in your personal and spiritual life.

The potential truly exists for you to have all the money you want. The potential exists for you to have the loving relationships you desire. The potential exists for you to have the healthy body that will be the foundation of your longevity and productivity. The potential exists for you to satisfy all the desires that God has placed within your heart. With these new habits, you could have more physical stamina. You could take advantage of new opportunities and cultivate new friendships. You could have a much more successful career. You could have the satisfaction that comes from serving God and the happiness that flows from the fulfillment of all your personal dreams.

If you would be willing to follow my program for just 13 weeks while focusing exclusively on one new habit during that timeframe, I promise you that you can develop the kind of beneficial behaviors that truly change your life, and you can do it without creating an unrealistic list of New Year's resolutions that never seem to "stick."

For years, people thought the magic timeframe for learning a new habit was 21 days. Others have offered different numbers that are supposed to lead to success. But B.J. Fogg, director of the Persuasive Technology Lab at Stanford University, says there's no magic time interval for making a new habit permanent.

"The speed of the habit formation is directly connected to the strength of the emotions you feel," Fogg explains. "It has nothing to do with 21 days."

That's why research conducted by University College London revealed that a new habit takes, on average, about 66 days to form. And, with that in mind, I like to allow myself 13 weeks (approximately 90 days) to establish a new habit in my life. I like 13 weeks because it gives me a little more than the "average" amount of time to solidify my new behavior. That timeframe just works out well for me. By adopting it, I give myself three dedicated months to nail down the new habit I want to establish, and I can do this precisely four times in a calendar year.

So, what new habits would you like to form? Do you want to start praying at least 20 minutes each day? Do you want to start flossing your teeth? Do you want to start writing personal notes to your new clients, your top prospects, or the people who are important to you in your life? Do you want to create a better system for managing your money and paying your bills? By adding not a colossal new goal but just one little behavior to your repertoire of repetitive activities over the next 13 weeks, you could dramatically improve your life and radically alter the course you are traveling. In fact, you could completely rewrite the storyline of your life and start laying the foundations for a legacy that could impact your family and friends for generations to come.

Let's get started. Pick the first habit you want to create, and pick the day you want to start working on it. Then, do four things before you actually begin.

- One, break that new habit down into its simplest component. I want you to break it down into the first "baby step" you need to take in order to start practicing the behavior in a deliberate way.
- Two, come up with some "cues" or "reminders" you can use to prompt this new behavior in your life. And try, if possible, to attach your reminders to habits you already perform.

- Three, create a "system" that will give structure to your habit formation. I want you to have a daily or weekly plan for getting from the bottom of the mountain to the top of the mountain in the 13 weeks you have allotted for your journey.
- And four, come up with a reward or a series of rewards that will make it worthwhile for you to practice your new behavior regularly.

Remember, the goal here is to create a natural system of motivation and response that will make your new behavior impossible to forget and easy to maintain. New Year's resolutions and vows to God are noble ideas, but they are driven by self-discipline and perpetuated through the force of sheer willpower, so they are doomed to fail once your determination grows weak or the tyranny of urgent distractions creeps into the picture and thrusts you back into your familiar routine. Like most people, you are not wired to say "no" to yourself for a long period of time, so anything born out of self-discipline is not designed to be permanent. However, actions prompted by natural reminders and sustained through instant incentives are much more likely to endure because a short period of focused intent (13 weeks) will yield a habit that should be permanently ingrained in your mind and subconsciously programmed into your behavioral patterns.

"INCHING" YOUR WAY FORWARD

So, right now, focus on the first habit you want to create. Figure out how to break that new behavior down into its simplest and easiest component. If you want to start flossing your teeth, for instance, start by flossing just one tooth. Seriously! That may sound a bit weird, but if you make the new behavior quick and easy in the beginning, you won't mind doing it. After you have flossed that single tooth long enough to make the behavior comfortable, it will be easy to start flossing more of your teeth—even all your teeth—without putting any pressure on yourself.

Before I go any further, maybe it would be a good idea to pause for a moment and help you understand why your first step in forming a new habit needs to be so easy. Obviously, you are anxious to achieve your objective. You are anxious to make this new behavior a permanent part of your life, and you are really "pumped up" with willpower and determination at this early stage of the process. So, you are cocked, wired, and ready to move forward as fast and as far as possible. You really want to get this done.

But, the most important thing as you take the initial steps toward making your new behavior permanent is to avoid failure at all costs. William James, the famed 19th century psychologist, said that a failure in the effort to perform a new behavior is a lot like dropping a ball of string. Each time you drop a ball of string, the string unwinds a little bit and you have to work hard just to rewind the string to where it was before you dropped it. You don't want to fail. You want to succeed. It would be better to floss one tooth and then dance around the bathroom in joyous celebration than it would be to floss all your teeth at the same time but choose to skip that new behavior the next night because it feels like it takes too much time.

We humans are just downright masterful at making excuses for ourselves. We can convince ourselves that we deserve a family-sized bag of potato chips after completing just one day of a diet, and we can convince ourselves that we don't need to floss our teeth every single night. But by starting your new behavior with the smallest and simplest step possible, you position yourself to recognize the psychological games that you play with yourself and resist the disruptive influence that these "mind games" have on your thinking. Besides, the goal in flossing just one tooth isn't to learn *how* to floss your teeth. Every person over the age of three knows how to floss his teeth. The goal is to *remember* to floss your teeth, and that goal will be much easier to achieve if you make the activity simple.

If you want to start eating more fruits and vegetables, begin by taking one sip of vegetable juice each morning when you take your daily vitamin. If you want to start running two miles each day, start by putting on your running shoes and then taking them off again. And, if you want to lose 40 pounds, begin by brushing your teeth immediately after dinner so you won't be tempted to snack after your evening meal. In other words, start really, really small. It is always better to take a tiny step forward and then savor the taste of victory than it is to take a giant leap forward only to fall back into a puddle of your own tears. Little successes become addictive, and that addiction to success can lead to bigger and better accomplishments down the road.

Also, try to think through the time of day you want to initiate this new habit. For instance, if you want to start reading one page in a self-help book with the goal of eventually reading a chapter each day, or if you want to start riding your bicycle once around the block with the long-range goal of riding five miles per day, think carefully about the time you set aside for this initial step in forming your new behavior. If you are a morning person, you will do better by getting your clothes and equipment together at night and going to bed 30 minutes earlier than usual so you can take advantage of your morning energy. If you try to ignore or override any deeply entrenched behaviors in order to create your new behavior, you will be creating unnecessary obstacles for yourself that will probably lead to your defeat.

Think this thing through before you actually get started. Make your first step so simple, so easy, and so closely aligned to the daily routines you now practice that you cannot possibly fail. Then, once you have determined the small step you want to take to get your new behavior up and rolling and how you intend to execute that initial step, try to come up with a strong "reminder" that will make it impossible for you to forget the behavior you want to perform.

One of the reminders I like to use when I'm developing a new habit is to write little notes to myself that I cannot possibly ignore throughout the day. For example, several years ago, when I became convinced that I needed to start drinking more water, I did some preliminary research and discovered that the typical person should drink about ten 8-ounce glasses of water each day. So, I put little "drink water" signs everywhere. I put them on my telephone, I put them on the dashboard of my car, I put them on my office door, I put them on my bathroom mirror, and, of course, I put them on my refrigerator. I even put one on my alarm clock, so it would be the first thing I saw each morning.

Now, I wouldn't want to live like this forever, sticking little post-it notes everywhere in my house and inside my office for other people to see. But the point of a reminder is to put something in front of your face that will stick out like a sore thumb and intrude upon your normal routines in an obvious and obscene way. After all, if you don't trip over it, you probably won't notice it, and if you don't notice it, you probably won't remember it. So, I usually make my reminders as noticeable as possible and as intrusive as possible, so I cannot possibly forget the behavior I am supposed to perform. Besides, the day will come when those post-it notes won't be necessary anymore. In the beginning, however, they are absolutely essential.

Another thing I did to remind myself to drink more water was to instruct my secretary to remind me every hour that I should be sipping on a glass of water. Overkill? Probably! But it worked. Few things are as effective in changing one's behavior as enlisting the help of others. Once we make ourselves accountable to other people, there is an added incentive for us to follow through with the actions we have decided to take.

I started with a single glass of water in the morning, and I evolved to the point where I was drinking water with all my meals (more about this shortly). By using all the little reminders that I incorporated into the process, I soon found myself drinking water all the time without even thinking about it. In fact, I quickly came to the place where I felt incomplete unless I had a bottle of water in my hand.

It goes without saying that I can't tell you the kinds of reminders that might work best for you. The reminders that you use to form your new habit will depend on the habit you are trying to form, the environment in which you are forming it, and your own personality and constraints. So, learn to be creative. That's all I can tell you. Regardless of the reminders you choose for yourself, give some careful consideration to the reminders you will use before you launch your efforts to create your new habit. You don't want to fail, because failure can lead to discouragement, and discouragement can lead to surrender. You want to succeed, and a couple of carefully chosen reminders can significantly increase your odds of success in this venture.

Do you want to start reading your Bible every morning before work? Then set your clock radio so you can wake up 30 minutes earlier than usual, and set the radio to a Christian station when you do. That way, you can wake up every morning to music that will remind you to read your Bible and inspire you to read it, as well.

Do you want to start brushing your teeth at night, as well as in the morning? Then after you have brushed your teeth in the AM, place your toothbrush on your pillow so you will be forced to look at it in the PM before you go to bed. Believe me, if you will do some small thing like this to interrupt your old patterns of behavior and remind yourself to perform your new behavior, your brain will soon get the message that you need to add an activity to your regimen of subconscious behaviors.

Be extreme. Be excessive. Be creative. Also be serious enough about nurturing your new habit that you would be willing to do something disruptive in order to remind yourself to do it. And make yourself accountable, if possible, to other people, because nothing can hold you to your new commitment quite like the watchful eye of another individual and the encouraging words of someone who wants you to succeed.

You need more, though, than a first step and a reminder to make you perform the behavior you want to learn. You also need a "system" that can help you move beyond your initial baby steps to the full-throttled execution of the activity you want to adopt. In other words, you need a plan. You need a strategy. You already know the tiny step you will be taking to introduce yourself to the behavior, but what will your second step be? And your third step? And your fourth? And how will you know when you have reached your final destination and the behavior has become permanent in your life?

I already shared with you my desire to start drinking 10 glasses of water each day, but I haven't shared with you the progression of steps that I took to get to my goal. To make things simple in the beginning so I could remember the behavior and assure my own success, I started with a single glass of water in the mornings. Each week, however, I "upped the ante." In addition to my morning glass of water, I started drinking water with all my meals. Then I started drinking water between each meal. Then I added a glass of water each night after dinner. Finally, I started drinking two glasses of water with each meal, bringing my total intake of water to ten glasses per day.

This means that step number one for me was a single glass of water in the mornings, step two was to add a single glass of water to each meal, step three was to add at least one glass of water between each of my meals, step four was to add a glass of water at night, and step five was to increase my intake to two glasses of water with each meal. By week five, therefore, I was already consuming ten glasses of water per day and was able to devote the next eight weeks to reinforcing my new behavior.

If you want to start flossing your teeth, your first step might be to floss just one tooth, and your second step might be to floss all your lower teeth. That means step three would be to floss all your teeth at the same time, upper and lower, leaving you with ten weeks to reinforce your new behavior.

Whether you are learning to drink water, floss your teeth, or pay your bills on time, I want you to devise some sort of progressive system that will help you start slowly and climb the ladder, one rung at the time, until you finally reach your goal. There is no right way or wrong way to do this, so the system you create and the timeframe you adopt are completely up to you (within your 13-week allotted period).

What isn't up to you, however, is the incremental approach you need to weave into your system because, as you know from your failed efforts to follow through with your New Year's resolutions, it is really hard to jump over a mountain with one gigantic leap. However, by taking a whole bunch of tiny steps that are really simple to perform, you will eventually get to the summit.

I cannot emphasize this enough. Most people who fail in their efforts to create new habits fail for one of two reasons. They fail because they don't make the behavior easy to perform in the beginning, or they fail because they don't think about the incremental steps they need to take to get to their final goal. And because they try to take big steps too fast, they often overlook the barriers that will arise to frustrate them along the way and force them to give up.

Best-selling author and financial advisor Ramit Sethi tells about the time when he was trying to develop the habit of going to the gym regularly in the mornings. For a while, Sethi's efforts paid off. He was waking up earlier than usual each morning and making the trek to the gym for a satisfying workout. But it wasn't long before Sethi got frustrated and decided to quit, and that's when he started thinking about why he had failed in his efforts to make this new behavior permanent. Sethi explains, "When I sat down to analyze why I wasn't going to the gym, I realized: my closet was in another room. That meant I had to walk out in the cold (to) put on my clothes. It was easier to just stay in bed. Once I realized this, I folded my clothes and shoes the night before. When I woke up the next morning, I would roll over and see my gym clothes sitting on the floor. The result? My gym attendance soared by over 300 percent."

Sethi recognized a barrier (an added step) that was causing him to fail. Instead of abandoning his hopes of making his new behavior habitual, he just thought of a way to turn that added step into a reminder. Wouldn't it have been easier for him if he had thought about this detail before he started? Or, wouldn't it have been wiser to actually "rehearse" his processes a time or two before doing them for real? Sethi came perilously close to throwing in the towel and walking away from his new behavior because he had failed to thoroughly plan the process. Before you start the process of learning a new habit, therefore, make sure you have planned and visualized every step you will need to take to make the behavior habitual and every step you will need to take to make the behavior permanent. That's what I did.

Before I started my 13-week program of increasing my water consumption, I had already decided what my first step would be (just one glass of water first thing in the morning). Before I started my program, I had already decided what my reminders would be (post-it notes and gentle nudges from my secretary and my wife). Before I took my first tiny step, I had already planned my incremental system of reaching ten glasses of water per day (by increasing my water intake gradually for five weeks and then maintaining that behavior for the next eight weeks). And before I approached the start date for my 13-week effort, I had given a lot of thought to the way I wanted the process to unfold so I could proactively eliminate any barriers to the simple execution of my new behavior that might become stumbling blocks in my effort to nurture that behavior.

I also gave a lot of thought to the final thing I needed to consider before starting the hard work of creating my habit. I gave a lot of thought to the rewards that I would utilize to make my new behavior repeatable. That's the final step you need to take in planning your success. You need to think about the "payoff" you will give yourself for doing a good job. After all, the thing that makes a habit permanent is the reward that makes it worthwhile. That's why I spent time planning my rewards the same way I spent time planning everything else about the process.

For one thing, I decided to remind myself each evening of how successful I had been that day. I decided to simply glance into my mirror and remind myself each night that I was going to be healthier for my efforts and more successful because of my faithfulness to my plan. In addition to these psychological pep talks, I also planned to incorporate my wife and my secretary into the process, because I knew they would fulfill two purposes for me without even realizing their roles. They would remind me to perform my new behavior, and they would reward me with praise when I did.

The emotional rewards of my efforts were plentiful and gave me the incentive I needed to stick with the plan on those less-than-inspiring days when the plan seemed hard to follow. To add to my arsenal of inducements and enticements, I also decided to reward myself at the end of each day with a snack of my choice. This made all that water a whole lot easier to swallow (pun intended).

FOUR STEPS TO SUCCESS

Do you have a habit in mind that you would like to create and imbed in your regimen of behaviors? Do you have a habit in mind that you would really like to incorporate into your life, yet which intimidates you every time you think about it?

1) Then first, think of the smallest step you could take to get started toward your goal.
2) Then, create one or more "reminders" that can keep the new behavior in the forefront of your conscious thoughts. When the behavior finally becomes habitual, you won't have to remind yourself to do it. However, until the behavior is branded into the subconscious parts of your brain, you will have to remind yourself to complete the behavior every time you need to perform it.
3) After that, devise the "system" you will use to get from your initial "baby step" to the full implementation of the behavior. Look beyond the first step to the bigger picture of your goal, determining what you want your habit to look like after it is

fully developed. Then create an incremental approach for getting there.

4) Finally, develop the "rewards" that will give you the incentive to follow the plan to completion. Remember, your mind and your body won't work for free. They are not your indentured servants. They want to be paid for what they do. So, before you even start the process of nurturing your new habit, you need to think about the incentives you can utilize to coax your body into performing it and the rewards you need to employ to make it worthwhile for your brain to absorb it.

The habits you now have in your life were formed through this proven process of habit formation, even though you were probably unaware that the process was taking place. This means that your new habits will have to be formed in the same way if you want them to become permanent and strong like the bad habits you wish you could shed. While your existing habits followed this pattern subconsciously, your desired habits will have to be nurtured intentionally. You will have to make this approach to habit formation work for you by strategy and design.

I'm not going to lie to you: The bad news is that good habits are hard to form. Until a habit becomes a habit, it takes a certain amount of self-discipline to instill that behavior in your life. But, after the behavior becomes habitual through repeated performance, the momentum keeps the process going, and the behavior becomes instinctive. The rationale behind my 13-week system is that, by repeating a behavior frequently and rewarding yourself for doing it, you will soon make the behavior automatic, and you won't have to rely on self-discipline any longer.

The good news is this: The principles I have shared with you work. Based on the proven science of subconscious habit formation, this system of reminders and rewards and calculated reprogramming is the best method I know for creating new habits in your life. If you want your brain to help you instead of oppose you, and if you want your body to remember the behaviors you are trying to learn, you are going to have to approach habit formation according to the way God created you. You are going to have to rely on the habitual aspects of your human nature to make beneficial behaviors repetitive.

I wish I could be more specific with some of the guidance I have offered here. I wish I could take every habit you might want to develop and walk you through a personalized program of reminders and rewards. I wish I could help you devise your systems so you can stick with your plan until the new habit is formed and strengthened. Unfortunately, every person will have a different goal regarding his or her life, and every person will have a different list of habits that he (or she) wants to cultivate in an effort to achieve those goals.

If you can't think of any, I can suggest some habits for you. In fact, in the next chapter (the final chapter), I want to give you a rather thought-provoking list of some of the good habits you may want to adopt. I can recommend some habits for you, but you must decide which habits you want to create, and you must determine the reminders, rewards, and systems that you can best utilize to make those habits permanent.

You are the one who will have to do the creative part of this equation. I have given you the guidelines, and I have given you some examples from my own experience and the experiences of others. But you are going to have to employ the truths I have shared with you as you determine the four habits you want to nurture and the creative ways you will go about implementing the things you have learned. You will have to take the helm of your own ship and turn the rudder, so you can steer that ship exactly where you want it to go. You will have to walk the walk so you can tell the tale afterward.

CHAPTER 8

HABITS WORTH HAVING

Your net worth to the world is usually determined by what remains after your bad habits are subtracted from your good ones.
Benjamin Franklin

EARLIER IN THIS BOOK, I SPENT SOME TIME comparing the bad habits of unproductive people with the good habits of effective people. In chapter four, where I elaborated on the ten behaviors that mark the lives of the world's most accomplished people, I attempted to demonstrate how life's most sought-after qualities are developed as a result of habit, not as a result of heredity or circumstance. Families that teach good habits are equipping their children for success, and individuals who acquire good habits are posturing themselves for greatness.

Specifically, I explained how successful people live focused lives, how they view the world around them with an optimistic attitude, and how they face adversity with a sense of resiliency. I explained how great people create positive associations, how they exhibit selflessness in their daily lives, and how they practice proper intimacy in all their meaningful relationships. I demonstrated how they maintain spirituality in a secular world, how they rely on order and method to keep themselves on track, and how they work to create physically healthy lifestyles. I also told you how these people work to live genuine lives, not virtual lives based on fantasy or the need to escape.

Successful people just don't fool around. Oh, they have their fun alright, and they know how to sleep in or "veg out" right along with the rest of us. But these needed escapes are planned, and they are infrequent and special for people with a driving purpose. Successful people live the brunt of their lives routinely doing those things that average people just won't do, and that is what makes them successful. Their lifestyle habits set them apart.

Olympic gold medalists, CEOs of major corporations, and Hall of Fame recording artists didn't make it to the top of their respective fields by doing the things that ordinary people do. That doesn't mean that they *never* did any of the things that the rest of us do. Of course, they had hobbies. Of course, they had friends. Of course, they did things on their climb to the top that you or I or anybody else would do from time to time to relax. But when the sun rose on a typical day in the lives of these individuals, the sun rose to find them doing things that would set them apart from others. Fishing isn't the primary focus of people who change the world; fishing is an occasional pastime of accomplished people and so is every other "nonproductive" activity. A sense of purpose and the specific vision that flows from that purpose are the passionate pursuits of great people, and these things determine the habits that these great people forge.

For instance, my primary motivation in life is to help people understand principles of success that are based on the Bible. With that purpose in mind, one of my principal goals is to become a best-selling author. That means that, in order to achieve my goal of writing books and in order to fulfill my God-given purpose of helping people grow, I have to nurture the kinds of habits in my life that will be in line with my purpose, habits that will help me do what I really want to do with my life. In this final chapter, therefore, I want to move beyond the broad characteristics that I described in chapter four, and I want to focus more on the specific habits you need to practice in order to achieve the things you really want to achieve with your life. Great people are willing to do things that "average" people aren't.

What is it that beats within your heart? What is it that you want to do or be more than anything else in the world? I want to put the final coat of paint on the subject of habit formation by sharing with you some practical illustrations of the kinds of daily behaviors that are part of a winning formula. Plus, I want to give you an extensive list of some of the tiny habits that can yield big results in your life if you will incorporate those habits into your routines by following the system I shared with you in the previous chapter.

HABITS OF REST

This may seem like a strange place to start, but people who are driven to do great things usually have more difficulty resting than they do working. In fact, highly motivated people tend to work themselves to exhaustion. Unfortunately, over time, the lack of rest can do as much harm to a person's body and soul as a lack of work can do to a person's bank account.

God made us to rest. As strange as it may seem, God Himself rests. The Bible tells us that God created the heavens and the earth in six days. Then, "on the seventh day he rested from all his work" (Genesis 2:2, NIV). So, to drive home the importance of rest, God modeled the concept of rest for us. Then He made rest one of the Ten Commandments, informing the Jewish people that He expected them to shut down the machinery of their lives one day each week and to make the Sabbath the centerpiece of their covenant with Him (see Exodus 31:16).

By the time Jesus came along, some 1500 years after God gave this commandment to the Jews, the definition of "rest" had been completely obscured. The Pharisees (a sanctimonious Jewish sect that existed around the time of Christ) told people that they weren't resting adequately unless they basically sat still all day. God never intended the Sabbath to be an affliction or an additional burden; He intended the Sabbath to be a day when people could simply set aside their work in order to sleep, play, worship with their loved ones, or just take a day off from the physical labor and emotional strain of their everyday lives. You, too, need to learn to rest. If you want to be happy and healthy, you need to learn to rest physically and you need to learn to rest mentally. The best way to do both of these things is to develop the kinds of habits that will help you do them.

Obviously, too much rest can be just as bad as no rest at all because too much rest can lead to laziness and poverty while too much work can lead to exhaustion, poor health, and failed relationships. The key is to find the proper balance in your life so you can be happy, healthy, and prosperous all at the same time. When it comes to the physical aspects of rest, therefore, you should consider devising some "systems" in your life that will give you some time to enjoy your favorite hobby or some occasional days just to sleep in or wrestle with the kids under the sheets.

What kind of rest do you need in your life specifically? As you plan the four habits you want to develop during the year ahead, how does rest fit into that picture? Do you need to step away from your workplace and spend more time with your family? Do you need to start planning a weekly "date night" with your spouse? Do you need more "down time" for yourself or more "fellowship time" with other Christians? Do you need an established day off each week? Do you need to join a spa, take an annual vacation, or start a new hobby? What exactly do you need to do to get the rest that you need because rest is a vital part of your well-being?

Rest is good for the body, but rest can be more than just the absence of physical labor. Rest can be playing a game of tag football in the backyard with your children. It can be a hike up a steep hill with a 10-pound backpack. It can be a grueling day of dirt riding on your motorcycle. Rest is simply the abandonment of all your normal responsibilities in favor of some time where you can do what you feel like doing, whether that means running a 5K race or snoring the day away in a dark bedroom.

If you want to be successful in life and if you want to remain strong and sane, make sure you create some habits that enable you to rest regularly. Close your business for a few hours, disable the phones, shut down the computers, and breathe some of that life-giving fresh air you've read about on the internet. Find something that meets your needs and your lifestyle, and just give it a rest.

HABITS OF GOOD HEALTH

I have already explained to you how successful people give attention to their health, focusing especially of their eating habits and their sleep. Accomplished people know that health is a gift from God that should be cherished and protected. Health isn't a "right" that is guaranteed for everyone, so high achievers make sure they do what is necessary to preserve their physical bodies.

What are some of the habits we should think about nurturing in order to create a healthy lifestyle? What are the behaviors we should seek to emulate in order to stay strong, alert, and free from sickness and pain?

None of us can control the aging process no matter how hard we try. Sometimes injury or affliction can invade our lives regardless of the precautions we take to protect ourselves from such things. But research proves that people can lower their odds of being sick or disabled if they do some basic things that are conducive to a long and healthy life.

For starters, a person should keep his (or her) weight in check, because obesity is a proven fast track to sickness. Obesity is also one of the most controllable causes of sickness there is. The idea of weight reduction means that exercise is somewhere on the horizon, and it means that responsible eating habits are a future requirement for you, as well. Perhaps at least one of your 13-week habits should be a habit involving diet or exercise.

Dietary changes, of course, should be incremental, and they should be reasonable. People who make New Year's resolutions to lose 40 pounds usually don't succeed. People who vow on December 31 to dramatically reduce their cholesterol usually don't stick with their oaths for more than a couple of days because sudden and dramatic changes rarely work, especially when it comes to our appetites. But you would be amazed how many changes you could make to your diet if you would devise a plan to make those changes slowly. You would also be amazed how many physical activities you could incorporate into your daily routine if you could find a way to make those activities fun.

In the past seven days, I have lost 10 pounds. I didn't lose that weight by doing something extreme or torturous. I simply started focusing on a couple of new habits I have been trying to incorporate into my life. I started eating more slowly, so I could give my stomach time to feel full. I learned to say "no" to sweets. And I learned to eat at certain times of the day in order to take advantage of my natural metabolism.

I also have a friend who lost 40 pounds rather easily. It took him almost a year to get the weight off, but he found it relatively painless to lose that weight because he did it slowly, using one of those diet programs that are currently being touted on television. My friend didn't try to radically change his diet on January 1, and he didn't try to totally eliminate the foods that he enjoys. He simply used a proven diet program (his "system") to help him learn how to incorporate healthier foods into his diet. When those foods became a habitual part of his diet, the unhealthy foods became less and less appealing to him, so my friend dropped 40 pounds in about 10 months.

However, if you fail to plan when it comes to your diet, then you are planning to fail, because healthier eating won't happen by accident. It won't happen because you want it to happen or because you occasionally order a salad with your barbecue spare ribs. If you want to increase your water intake, decrease your sodium, increase the vegetables you eat, decrease the sugary products you consume, increase your fiber, or decrease your calories or cholesterol, you are going to have to develop a reasonable plan for achieving these goals in bite-sized pieces (pun intended). And you are going to have to incorporate "reminders" and "rewards" into the process. If you don't, you will fail. I promise.

The same goes for exercise. To a lot of people, the idea of exercise seems like a death sentence. But exercise can be easier than running in place on a treadmill at a crowded gym five miles from your house, and it can be more fun than a brisk walk by yourself around the same block you have navigated a million times in the past. Exercise can include rock climbing, dancing, cycling, martial arts, and rough-housing with the kids. It can even involve video games that make you get up and move around.

The key is to find some kind of activity that is fun for you. If you like being around people, you can even make the activity a social event. Playing basketball with your friends or playing "Just Dance" with your children can be a lot more fun than almost anything you can imagine. Once again, be creative. Do some thinking before you do some moving. Devise a plan that will lead to your reasonable and achievable goals, whether those goals involve your sleep habits, your eating habits, your exercise habits, or your posture. And instead of defying your needs for companionship and fun, incorporate those needs into your regimen. Give yourself a chance to succeed by giving yourself a chance to enjoy what you do.

HABITS OF ORGANIZATION

In chapter four, I mentioned that successful people tend to be organized. But, what does that mean, exactly? Can disorganized people really get themselves organized? It's not in their genes. Or … is it?

This is one of my "pet peeves" in life, and it's one of my wife's pet peeves, as well. We have busy lives and a lot of individual and shared responsibilities. We are passionate about organization because disorganization wastes more time and money than just about anything else in the world.

Think about it! In a typical month, how much time do you spend organizing your life? Now, in comparison, how much time do you spend putting out "fires"? I challenge you to live just one day without investing time or money in solving a problem that resulted from your own lack of organization.

In this regard, businesses are just like individuals. In business as in our personal lives, we spend far too much time redoing the things we could have done right the first time if we had created a "system" before performing that task. But we humans don't like to "waste time" organizing things. Instead, we prefer to just dive headfirst into the swimming pool because we are convinced that we can fill the pool with water at a later time. Unfortunately, this approach to life forces us to invest twice the time and three times the money to do just about everything we do.

How many times, for instance, have you made two trips to the same store in the same week? How many times have you purchased something you couldn't find in your kitchen drawer only to find that item the next day in the glove compartment of your car? How many times have you apologized to someone for forgetting a birthday or another important date or appointment? How many times have you searched for an item of clothing you really wanted to wear only to find that item a week later beneath a pile of clothes on a chair in your bedroom?

We can't remember things, we can't find things, and we can't do things right the first time because we don't organize the simplest activities in our lives. Rather, we tend to be "reactive." We chase after this little disaster over here or pour water on that little fire over there. As a result of this chaotic approach to living, we never seem to get things done, and we never seem to have time for the things that really matter to us. The problem with living this way—focusing on what is urgent instead of what is important—is that it causes us to waste the full potential of our lives.

Fortunately, just a little bit of organization can change this careless pattern. For instance, hanging up your clothes immediately after taking them off could enable you to have something appropriate to wear on a moment's notice and make your chaotic mornings a lot less stressful. Or keeping a little book of postage stamps in the side pouch of your toiletry bag could keep you from searching for stamps while you are traveling far from home.

As you think about the new habits you want to form this coming year, consider some habits that will bring more order to your life. Maybe your finances need to be organized so you know exactly what you make, exactly what you spend, and exactly what you need to be doing from year to year to prepare for the future. Maybe your work needs to be better organized, so you can stay a step ahead of your competition instead of dealing with the chaos every day. Perhaps you need to start with smaller things. Maybe you just need to organize the drawers in your kitchen. Maybe you need to vacuum the French fries from between the seats in your car.

Give some thought to those areas of your life that bring you frustration because these are the areas that create disorder for you and for others. Start paying attention to what is robbing your space, robbing your money, and robbing your time every day, and you will quickly realize that these are the areas that need more order and regularity. Then, once you start noticing the parts of your life that need to be better organized, you can put that new habit on your list.

Little in life will bring you a greater return on investment than organizing your records, your calendar, your living space, or your professional activities. Nothing in life will help you travel more easily to where you want to go than organizing your approach to the journey ahead.

HABITS OF PLANNING

While we are thinking about the benefits of organization, we should realize that the organization of time is perhaps the most important type of organization there is. We waste so much time by wandering into the future like blind men in a maze when just a little bit of advanced planning could make the journey so much more enjoyable and so much more productive.

Here's a great illustration of what I'm talking about: In 2013, CBS News reported on a study conducted by the Federal Reserve Bank of New York. In that study, the researchers found that only 27 percent of college graduates are currently working in a field directly related to their college majors. That means that 73 percent of college graduates end up wandering their way into a professional career instead of planning to enter that career and preparing for it.

To be fair, I know that unforeseen things can occur in life. Entire sectors of the economy can shut down or become obsolete. I also know that 18-year-old college freshmen aren't always prepared to plot out the rest of their lives with absolute certainty. But this kind of haphazard approach to life isn't confined to 18-year-olds. According to the *Wall Street Journal* (September 4, 2010), the average American worker will have seven different careers in his or her lifetime.

Things happen, and we have to learn to adjust to the changes that occur in life. But, most of the chaos in our lives is not chaos that is rooted in the external and uncontrollable things that happen to the economy or the world around us; most of the chaos is our lives is self-generated. We just don't plan for things. We don't plan our careers, we don't plan for retirement, and we don't plan for eternity. Heck, we don't even plan our own meals very well. We waste a lot of time and money suffering the consequences of our own lack of forethought.

Earlier in this book, I shared with you how one woman I know purchases a Christmas gift for each of her friends and family members whenever she buys that person's birthday gift or birthday card each year. That way, her holiday shopping is finished well in advance without any stress and without any difficulty. The point I was trying to make by sharing that little story is that we can do things like this in all the routine matters of life.

If you think about it, almost all of life's responsibilities are predictable or cyclical. We all know we are going to die, so why do we avoid planning our estates? We all know we are going to retire (unless we die first), so why do we wait until we are 60 years old before thinking about our latter years? We all know we are going to have careers, we are probably going to get married, and we are probably going to have children. So, why are we always so unprepared for these things? Modern Americans like to think that somehow "everything will just work itself out." But most things don't work themselves out; we have to work them out. We should never forget, therefore, that the holidays are cyclical, the seasons are cyclical, tax season is cyclical, and the summertime, when the kids are out of school, is an annual thing.

These things happen with regularity and at predictable times of the year. We should never allow foreseeable things to sneak up on us and sucker punch us.

I understand that, because of God's grace, portions of our lives can often work themselves out without a lot of planning. But a quality life doesn't happen by accident. People who live "abundant" lives do so because they plan their lives, especially those parts of their lives that matter most to them. They don't take life for granted. Perhaps you need to add one or two habits to your list that involve some sort of planning, because planning is the very first step to success in any endeavor.

Do you have financial goals for the coming year? What are your plans for achieving those goals? Do you have health goals for the coming year? What are your plans for making them happen? I know a lot of successful people, and many of these people "plan to plan." That's right! They actually plan time to sit down so they can plan the things they want to do. They block off time in their schedules just to think about how they are going to do the things they are planning to do. Perhaps you should do the same. Perhaps you should develop a habit of sitting down once a week to plan the week ahead and beyond.

I read an article recently about a powerful businessman who begins each day by just lying in his bed and thinking for 30 minutes each morning. That's right! As soon as he wakes up, he spends a half-hour under the covers thinking about the day ahead and what he wants to do with it.

I also have a friend who sits down every summer to start working on a calendar for the upcoming year, and he puts all kinds of things on that calendar! He puts the major sporting events that he wants to watch, he blocks off his vacation dates, so he can safeguard his personal and family time, and he writes down birthdays and anniversaries, so he can be sure he reaches out to the key people in his life on their special days. He even puts license renewal dates on his calendar and due dates for government filings that are associated with his business. Another thing my friend includes on his annual calendar are those things he wants to accomplish during the year ahead. He takes the goals he wants to achieve and breaks those goals down into 12 monthly or 52 weekly processes, and then he completes those various processes one at the time until he reaches the goal he established for himself.

This plan to do some planning has actually saved my friend a lot of time and money over the years and has enabled him to achieve things he might otherwise never have achieved. Planning, therefore, is a way to avoid trouble, and planning is a way to take advantage of opportunity. Planning is everything, and that is why you need to plan your days before you engage them, plan your weeks before they start, plan your years before you live them, and plan your life if you want to control its outcome. Think about nurturing some habits that can help you in this regard.

HABITS OF TIME MANAGEMENT

In their 1994 book, *First Things First*, Stephen Covey and Robert Merrill presented a two-by-two matrix that could help any person better manage his or her time. On the vertical plane of this matrix are the "urgent" and "not urgent" things that consume a person's time. On the horizontal plane are the "important" and "not important" things that consume time.

	Urgent	Not Urgent
Important	Crying baby Kitchen fire Some calls 1	Exercise Vocation Planning 2
Not Important	3 Interruptions Distractions Other calls	4 Trivia Busy work Time wasters

Merrill and Covey suggested that people should use this matrix at the start of each week to plan the main events in their lives for the upcoming week. The first quadrant (urgent and important) should contain those preplanned events that are the most pressing for the week ahead. The second quadrant (not urgent but important) are things that will matter significantly in the long run, but probably won't yield any results in the immediate future. The third quadrant (urgent but not important) are all the things that pop up during the week that require immediate attention, yet which produce practically nothing for the bottom line of one's life. And the fourth quadrant (not urgent and not important) contains all the activities that are the mindless, unproductive things people do simply because they need a break from the normal routines of life.

If you want to be successful, the creation of a weekly matrix like this could turn your life around. By setting aside a little time one day toward the end of each week to plan the week in front of you, you could save a lot of wasted time and actually move your life forward in measurable ways. So, if time management is one of the new habits you would like to form, let me tell you right up front that you *cannot* control the first quadrant and you *must* control the fourth quadrant. Controlling the second and third quadrants are the difference between excellence and mediocrity. The third quadrant is your biggest enemy because these are the activities that consume all your time yet produce nothing for you and make you feel like you are getting nowhere with your life.

The second quadrant, however, is as beneficial to a successful life as the third quadrant is threatening. The activities in the second quadrant (like relationship building and continual education) won't produce immediate benefits for you. But, while neglecting them can lead to long-term failure, valuing them will definitely lead to greater success. Therefore, because they do not produce immediate rewards, be careful not to neglect them or postpone them. Instead, work to make these behaviors habitual in your life.

As we plan for the days, weeks, months, and years ahead of us, we should have a matrix like this in front of us, or we should have some other strategy that can help us block off the time we need to give due attention to the things that truly matter. This is the essence of effective time management. But if we fail to manage our time, our time will evaporate in front of our eyes, and the things that are utterly meaningless in this world will slowly devour all our precious years while leaving us empty and unfulfilled in the end.

HABITS OF MONEY MANAGEMENT

How much money do you waste? How much stress does money create for you? How much more money could you be earning if you were a better steward of your talents and resources? How many financial problems could you have avoided over the course of your life if you had been more aware of how money works? Next to health, I don't know of any other area of life that causes people more concern than money. For this reason, you need a lot of good financial habits if you intend to live a prosperous and less stressful life.

Many people waste a lot of money because they are poor planners. You could save thousands on a new automobile, for instance, if you could wait until the right time of the year to buy your new car. You could save hundreds on furniture by purchasing it at the right time of the year. How about your insurance policies? Do you ever review them or shop around for a better deal from some of your provider's competitors? Even medical costs can differ by 100 percent or more from one provider to the next, but many people never take the time to shop or to plan.

I realize that it is impractical to shop around for every can of beans you buy. However, you could certainly shop for the big-ticket items that you purchase infrequently, and you could certainly reevaluate your long-term financial commitments once a year to make sure you're not missing out on a better deal. Yet, in order to do these things, you have to be organized, and you have to have a plan.

Many people also waste a lot of money because they don't take the time to learn how money works. They simply pull out a credit card to buy just about everything they need, never giving a thought to how interest compounds against them and how that interest could work in their favor if they would ever make the journey from the borrower's side of the fence to the investor's side.

Do you realize that if you bought a simple furniture ensemble for $1,750 and put that payment on a credit card (18 percent annual percentage rate), it would take you more than 22 years to pay for that furniture by making the minimum monthly payment? That's right! If you just made the minimum monthly payment, it would take you more than 22 years to pay for that sofa and chair, which, by that time, would be in a landfill somewhere. And you would pay $3,647 in interest just for the privilege of borrowing that $1,750. So, your $1,750 sofa and chair would actually end up costing you about $5,397. What a waste!

However, by adding just $25 per month to your minimum payment, you could pay for that sofa and chair in a little more than 3 years. Instead of paying $3,647 to the bank for the privilege of using its money, you could pay the bank just $588 instead. That is the power of discipline. That is the power of knowledge. That is the power of compound interest working in your favor. You can't win the game though, if you don't know the rules, and you can't take advantage of the rules if you don't make a habit of learning the rules and applying them to your life.

How about your earning potential? Do you keep a resume out there, circulating in your professional arena just in case there might be a better position for you with a different company? Do you take time periodically to review your schedule to find out how you might start using some of your free time to earn additional income while doing something you enjoy?

All these things are possible for the person who develops the right habits. A person who is good at money management is a person who regularly considers the things he is doing today while regularly investigating in the things he wants to do tomorrow. He (or she) is constantly exploring new products, new providers, and more cost-effective ways of doing routine things at work and at home. He (or she) is constantly going through the household budget to question each expenditure and to contemplate ways of boosting revenues. Financial analysis is an "automatic" part of the prudent person's life.

Chaos and indifference are the two biggest enemies of economic prosperity. We waste what we have today because we don't balance our checkbooks regularly or pay our bills on time. We approach tomorrow unprepared for its opportunities and challenges because we never take the time to plan ahead or to think about the long-term consequences of today's financial choices.

As you contemplate the four new habits you want to create this coming year and the 20 new habits you want to create over the next five years, I hope some of your new habits will involve your finances because King Solomon said that "money is the answer for everything" (Ecclesiastes 10:19, NIV). That is, money can make your life a lot better. It can make your life happier, healthier, and less stressful while the lack of money can make your life a lot more difficult. The really sobering news is that your present financial condition is the result of the habits you had yesterday, but the good news is that your future will be the result of the financial habits you create today.

Please consider, therefore, some of the following money management habits:

- Monitoring your spending habits and modifying accordingly (noting every dollar you spend).
- Buying for price, not prestige (and learning to wait for the right time to buy).
- Guaranteeing your future by paying yourself first (saving the first 10 percent of your earnings).
- Setting a specific time each week to pay your bills (and creating a bookkeeping system to keep things organized).
- Establishing a budget and sticking with it (by limiting the cash you carry in your wallet).
- Establishing a retirement plan (and opening the necessary accounts).
- Starting your journey out of debt (by living on cash and putting all your extra money toward your smallest debt first).
- Checking your credit reports annually (and checking your Social Security statement, driving record, and mortgage report at the same time).
- Reviewing all your service contracts and insurance policies over the course of the year (and obtaining quotes from competitive providers).

I could give you many more suggestions, but I think you get the point. Nothing causes more misery in life than financial difficulties, while financial stability enables us to enjoy our lives and enrich the lives of others. A person's financial status is always a reflection of his or her past choices, so let the decisions you make today write a prosperous storyline for your future. Develop the habits you need in order to be financially independent and prosperous.

HABITS OF LEARNING

Most people have big televisions; successful people have big libraries. Accomplished people put time and energy into the process of increasing their knowledge. They read. They learn. They spend time with people who can teach them things they do not know already. They study, they analyze, and they think.

Too many people believe that the process of systematic learning ceased in their lives when they graduated from high school or college. But great people know that they will begin to wither as soon as they stop learning. We should all apply ourselves to the process of learning new things and attaining new levels of understanding.

What do you want to do with your life? If you know the answer to that question, you are farther down the road to success than most other people. If you know the answer to that question, let me ask you the next question that you need to consider, a question that will make the difference between achieving your goal and just wishing for it. The question is this: What is it that you need to know in order to make your dream a reality?

Once you know where you want to go with your life and once you know what you want to do, this follow-up question is the most important question you could ask yourself, because the only thing standing between you and that "thing" you want to achieve is a lack of information. The lack of knowledge is the greatest barrier between success and failure, yet most people don't even have enough knowledge to know how much they don't know.

Just slow down and think about this for a minute before you speed-read your way through the rest of this chapter. If you could go back in time and relive your life knowing what you know today, would you change anything? Of course, you would! That fact alone should show you that knowledge could have changed the course of your life. If you had known then what you know now, you would have done things differently and your life would have turned out differently. In the same way, the knowledge you gain today is able to change your life going forward.

Or think about it in these terms: When you need your car repaired, whom do you call? Or if you wake up with a strange pain in your stomach, where do you go to get relief from that pain? You go to a mechanic and pay him hundreds of dollars to fix your car because that mechanic knows things about automobiles that you simply do not know. You go to a doctor and pay him thousands of dollars to fix your stomach because that doctor knows things about the human body that you do not know.

If you could learn some things today that you didn't know yesterday, your tomorrows would look a whole lot different than they look right now. And for that reason alone, you may want to develop some new habits that will improve your base of knowledge or expand your wisdom. Let me recommend a few:

- If you are an early riser, you could start a habit of reading one chapter from the Bible or from a personal development book each morning before leaving for work or school.
- You could do some online advanced study in your professional field every evening instead of watching reruns of *I Love Lucy*, and you might even earn some certifications that could enhance your earning power.
- You could slowly learn a new language over the course of several years (perhaps visiting a country where they speak that language once you gain a reasonable level of proficiency).
- You could learn the technical side of a hobby you enjoy (such as golf club repair) and perhaps earn some extra income on the side.
- You could join a club or civic organization that is open to people in a particular field, so you can nurture relationships with people who can teach you things you need to know about an area of expertise that interests you.

The sky is the limit. You just need to be creative. For every desire you can identify within your own heart, there is a pathway you can walk to bring that desire to life. You just have to find the passion, figure out what you need to do to start chasing after it, and then create one new habit in your life that will help you gain the knowledge you need to get started on your journey. Once you start the journey, everything else will fall into place.

HABITS OF RELATIONSHIP BUILDING

Contrary to popular belief, relationships don't happen by accident. They aren't the result of "fate." Relationships are forged as a consequence of our habits. The places we go, the things we do, and the interests that consume us all have an influence on the people we meet. And the relationships we forge as a result of our habits will do more to shape our lives than we might imagine. For this reason, you may want to consider forming at least one new habit that will help you nurture some healthy relationships in your life.

As I explained earlier, the people around you will slowly shape you. These people will create both a "floor" and a "ceiling" for your life. They won't allow you to descend so low that you become an embarrassment to them or a drag on their lives, but they won't allow you to rise so high that you leave them behind in the dust either. Consequently, you should seek to surround yourself with people who think positively, speak positively, and behave in ways that are conducive to your growth and success, because, if you spend all your time with people who are going nowhere with their lives, you will go nowhere with them.

Just think about it! This fact of life is true for two reasons. First, your friends won't feel comfortable being around you if you are behaving in ways that are beneath them or in ways that make them feel beneath you. At the same time, you will feel uncomfortable spending all your time around people who make you feel like you are out of your "element." If you don't drink alcohol, for instance, you won't feel comfortable around people who drink a lot. And if you like to talk about the Lord, people who hate going to church won't feel comfortable around you.

So if you want to be great, you need to start thinking like other great people, and you need to start spending your time with the kind of people you want to emulate. If you want to be a success in business, for instance, you need to spend less time with people who are satisfied to spend their lives working for minimum wage, and you need to start spending more time with entrepreneurs and proactive thinkers.

You may also need to change your speech patterns. Negative people, who view everything through a negative filter, tend to spew negative words from their mouths constantly. Positive people, who see potential in almost every situation, tend to speak words that lift up instead of tear down, words that encourage people rather than crushing them. To get closer to great people who can lift you up and propel you forward, you may need some new habits of conversation. And the irony here is that the more positive you become with your words, the more the world's "winners" will want to spend time with you, but the more negative you become in your speech, the harder it will be to attract successful people to you.

Ironically, the good relationships that can help you forge better habits won't arise in your life unless you form some good habits first, habits that are conducive to relationship building because all of us by nature are drawn to the path of least resistance. We are not inclined to "stretch" ourselves too much or to do things that will make us uncomfortable. Consequently, you need to take the first step to make new relationships possible in your life. You need to join an organization that will put you in touch with the kind of people you want in your life, or you need to start volunteering for a charity, so you can rub shoulders with people who think on a grander scale than the people you know right now.

I'm not saying you need to divorce yourself from your family or turn your back on your friends. What I am saying is that if you spend all your time with people who fail to lift you up, you will always stay where you are right now. In order to meet new people and make new friends, you need to develop some habits that will put you in places where you can cross paths with accomplished people. In other words, you need to start "networking."

No matter what your personal dreams may be, I can promise you that you will never achieve your dreams alone. You will need the advice, the help, the wisdom, and the constructive criticism that others can share with you as you strive to advance your cause. You will need to glean from others what you do not possess yourself. This is God's design for your life, so you can stay humble. Rest assured that these kinds of relationships won't happen by chance; they will happen because you took some steps to make these relationships possible. They will happen as a result of your habits. Then, to nurture the relationships that you forge, you will need additional habits that can help you strengthen your relationships and build them. For instance, you may need to learn these skills:

- Listen more and talk less.
- Ask questions instead of making statements.
- Remember the important things a person tells you about himself or herself.
- Manage your emotions in challenging situations.
- Be open and honest and be wise about how to do it.

Relationships are hard, but they are rewarding. Relationships are hard, but they are the building blocks of life, both your personal life and your professional life. Make the pursuit of new and rewarding relationships a strong focus of your habit formation.

HABITS OF GIVING

The most successful people tend to be the most generous people. Successful people give to worthy causes because successful people know that their success is attributable in part to the contributions that others have made to their lives. Consequently, these people want their success to contribute in meaningful ways to the betterment of others.

I believe in giving, but I do not believe in the concept of "giving back" to society for the success you have enjoyed because I don't believe that society makes people successful or unsuccessful. I believe that the society in which a person works is a lot like the soil in which a farmer plants his seeds. Good soil is more likely to produce a good harvest than bad soil, but good soil doesn't guarantee anything. It is still up to the farmer to make the soil work for him. In a region where good soil is available to everyone, ingenuity, creativity, personal sacrifice, and hard work are the differences that distinguish the prosperous farmer from the farmer who is forced into bankruptcy.

So "giving back" is not a viable notion, but simple giving for the sake of giving is both biblical and right because even though a person's success is largely dependent on his abilities and work habits, a successful person realizes that other people have played a role in his achievements. For instance, the politician who becomes president of the United States knows that he was supported and advised by countless people throughout his political career. The young pastor who eventually builds a large and influential church knows that he was mentored by a parent or other authority figure who poured sacrificially into that young pastor's life. And the businessman who seems to have a knack for turning opportunities into gold knows that he was taught the finer points of sales and financing, marketing and tax law, by the countless people who surrounded him during his professionally formative years.

These people realize that if it had not been for the contributions of others, they might still be struggling to get off the ground. They realize the important roles that other people have played in their success. Great people also understand the role that God has played in equipping them and directing their lives. This is the reason successful people tend to be big givers. They want to make other people's lives better the same way that other people helped make their lives better. They want to improve the world that gave them the opportunity to make life better for themselves.

As you contemplate the new habits you would like to form this coming year, you may want to make giving a part of your regimen. Perhaps you can start tithing to your church. Perhaps you can start mentoring others in the things that you know and do well. Perhaps you can lay aside your typical professional role for a couple of hours each week and get your hands dirty laboring beside other selfless people as a charity volunteer. Perhaps you can even set your sights on creating your own charity or charitable event that can raise money for the cause that tugs at your heart.

As you consider the new habits you want to establish in your life, don't let all of them focus on you and your needs. Give some thought to God, give some thought to your family, and give some thought to those who can benefit from your resources and expertise. The person who pours everything into himself is the person who will never be truly happy, but the person who allows his life to be a blessing to others is the person who can truly never fail.

HABITS OF PUTTING GOD FIRST

You don't have to be a committed Christian to be a giver, but you do have to be a giver to be a committed Christian. You also have to put God first in all the other areas of your life if you intend to be a devoted follower of Christ.

When that inevitable day comes, your physical death is imminent, and you start thinking about the life you have lived, you aren't going to care about the number of business deals you transacted during your career or the size of the boat you were able to buy. You aren't going to care about the lowest score you shot on the golf course or how well your investments did over the previous 12 months. In those final moments of your life, you are only going to think about three things. You are going to think about the legacy of the life you have lived. You are going to think about the people you have loved. And most of all, you are going to think about your stance with God as you prepare to meet Him.

If these are the three things that will really matter to you at the end of your life, shouldn't they be the same things that you focus on right now? If you know that the day is coming when these things will matter more to you than anything else, shouldn't they matter to you today?

As you contemplate the habits you need to form to improve the quality of your life, I encourage you to place your spiritual life at the top of that list. The good habits you could form to enhance your relationship with God are innumerable, and they encompass almost every aspect of your life. If you ever want God to be first in your life, you need to start making Him first right now.

If you are a Christian, you should read the Bible from cover to cover at least once in your life, preferably once a year. If you are a Christian, you need to spend some time alone with God on a regular basis (something we call "prayer"). If you are a Christian, you need to give, you need to serve, you need to talk to people about God, and you need to be as regular as possible in the house of the Lord. You need to spend time with people, encourage people, and get involved in people's lives. You need to make your talents available to your church, you need to participate in a ministry outreach at home or abroad, and you need to do some tangible and practical things to show your appreciation and support for those who care for you spiritually.

The beautiful thing about the Christian life is that God loves us whether we do these things or not. He saves us by faith whether we do these things or not. But when we come to know Him and when we come to experience His forgiveness and His presence in our lives, our natural response should be to do things that are pleasing to Him and spiritually beneficial for ourselves.

Besides, the really amazing thing about the Christian life is that the closer we get to the Lord, the closer we want to get. The more we do for God and others instead of ourselves, the more we want to do. Nothing can change your life and put you in a position to experience God's favor quite like honing habits that will build spiritual character in your soul and normalize positive Christian behaviors in your life.

While you create the list of habits you want to establish for yourself this coming year, consider your soul at least as much as you consider your body and your bank account. Once you form a habit, you could easily be stuck with that habit for the rest of your earthly life. So make sure you form habits that will bring you success today and satisfaction for the rest of your life and throughout eternity.

CLOSING THOUGHTS

If you found yourself in a situation where you were managing your own business and you needed to hire someone for an important position in your company, what habits would you look for in the person you wanted to hire? Would you look for someone who was disorganized or someone who had a reputation for meeting important deadlines? Would you look for someone who had a track record of shirking responsibility or someone who demonstrated qualities of leadership? Would you look for someone who was knowledgeable and well read or someone who just watched TV all the time? Would you look for a courteous employee or someone who would be short-tempered with your customers?

Every employer would prefer employees who have great work habits. If you know you would seek such qualities in the people you would hire, you should follow your own advice and start developing the kinds of habits that others will admire in you, habits that will help you produce the kind of life you want to live and the kind of results that will command the attention and respect of those you encounter along life's way.

If you can gain control of your own habits, you can gain control of your time. If you can gain control of your own habits, you can gain control of your health. If you can gain control of your own habits, you can gain control of your finances, your relationships, and your destiny. Life is too short not to make the most of it. So, start developing habits right now that will make tomorrow everything you ever dreamed it could be.

You will never rise above your habits, and your habits can make or break you. Your habits will dictate whether you succeed or fail in life. Therefore, if you want to be happy, if you want to be content, if you want to be fulfilled and balanced and pleased with yourself and with life, you need to develop a healthy array of habits because your success depends on your ability to display behaviors that can set you apart from the crowd and propel you forward in whatever you choose to do. Good habits are your stepping stones to greatness.

FOLLOW DR. DAVE!

 @drdavemartin

 @drdavemartin

/davemartininternational

 /thedrdavemartin

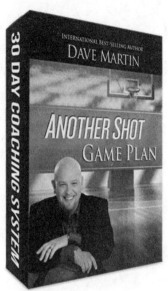

ANOTHER SHOT
GAME PLAN
30-DAY COACHING SYSTEM

EBOOK • AUDIOBOOK • WORKBOOK • COACHING VIDEOS

COACHES INCLUDE
**JOEL OSTEEN, PAT WILLIAMS, SAM CHAND,
SIMON BAILEY, AMYK HUTCHENS,
TERRI SAVELLE FOY...AND MANY MORE**

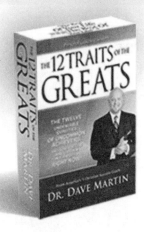

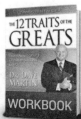

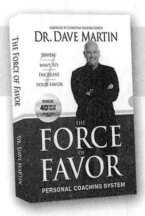

INSPIRE
IMPACT CULTURE. INFLUENCE CHANGE

INTRODUCING THE INSPIRE COLLECTIVE

While many churches are effective in equipping Christians for ministry within their walls, some struggle to prepare them for service in other arenas—their workplace, their neighborhood, their social community.

But the call to be change-makers is for all believers: Artists, business people, civic servants, community leaders, educators, mechanics, stay-at-home parents, students, and wait-staff.

That's why the Inspire Collective was established, to help raise up true influencers who are kingdom-focused Monday through Saturday, not just on Sundays.

The Inspire Collective delivers a unique blend of inspiration and application, spiritual and practical, for those wanting to impact and influence their everyday world for Christ.

THE INSPIRE COLLECTIVE OFFERS

- MAGAZINE
- BOOKS
- STUDY RESOURCES
- COURSES
- LIVE CLASSES
- EVENTS
- LOCAL NETWORKS

FOUNDED BY
Mike Kai, Martijn van Tilborgh, Sam Chand

.COM